The Social Anxiety Disorder Solution and Cognitive Behavioral Therapy

2 Books in 1

Retrain your brain to overcome shyness, depression, anxiety, panic attacks and find self confidence.

Written by:
Michael Cooper & George B. Wells

Michael Cooper & George B. Wells
© Copyright 2019 - All rights reserved.

The content contained within this book may not be reproduced, duplicated or transmitted without direct written permission from the author or the publisher.

Under no circumstances will any blame or legal responsibility be held against the publisher, or author, for any damages, reparation, or monetary loss due to the information contained within this book, either directly or indirectly.

Legal Notice:
This book is copyright protected. It is only for personal use. You cannot amend, distribute, sell, use, quote or paraphrase any part, or the content within this book, without the consent of the author or publisher.

Disclaimer Notice:
Please note the information contained within this document is for educational and entertainment purposes only. All effort has been executed to present accurate, up to date, reliable, complete information. No warranties of any kind are declared or implied. Readers acknowledge that the author is not engaging in the rendering of legal, financial, medical or professional advice. The content within this book has been derived from various sources. Please consult a licensed professional before attempting any techniques outlined in this book.

By reading this document, the reader agrees that under no circumstances is the author responsible for any losses, direct or indirect, that are incurred as a result of the use of information contained within this document, including, but not limited to, errors, omissions, or inaccuracies.

THE SOCIAL ANXIETY DISORDER SOLUTION

How to Overcome Shyness, Prevent Panic Attacks, and Find Self-Confidence (Includes Specific Solutions For Teens, Kids & Women)

Michael Cooper

Table of Contents

Introduction 9

Chapter 1: What is Social Anxiety? 15
   Do You Have Social Anxiety Disorder? 15
      Is Social Anxiety a Mental Disorder? 16
      Is Social Anxiety a Mental Disease? 18
      How Common is Social Anxiety? 20
   Does Social Anxiety Develop in Early Childhood? 20
   Social Anxiety in Children 22
      Anger Problems as an Indicator of SAD 23
      Paternal Role in Developing SAD 23
      Future Risk of Depression for Children with SAD 24
      Severe Fear, Anxiety and Rumination in Adulthood 24
   Gender Differences 25
   Causes of Social Anxiety 26
      Genetic Causes 26
      Parenting and Early Childhood 27
      Unsafe Environment 29
   Symptoms of Social Anxiety 30
   What Triggers Social Anxiety? 31
   SAD Symptoms Checklist 33

Chapter 2: Effects of Social Anxiety in Real Life 35
   How Does Social Anxiety Affect Your Life? 37
      Everyday Interactions 38

Physical Health 38
Family Life 39
Personal Relationships 40
Work 43
Depression and Social Anxiety 45
Eating Disorders 46
Social Anxiety and Autism 47
Types of Phobias 48
    Shyness, Social Phobia, and Avoidant
    Personality Disorder 49
    Types of Social Phobia 49

Chapter 3: Getting to Know Your Social Anxiety Disorder 51
Thoughts That Trigger Anxiety 58
Track Behaviors 61
Social Anxiety in Children and Adolescents 62
Workbook: SAD Thought Record Worksheet 63

Chapter 4: How to Overcome Shyness 68
What Makes You Shy? 70
    You Perceive Yourself Negatively 70
    You Put All Your Attention on You 72
What Happens to Your Mind and Body When
You Are Shy? 72
    Unrealistic Goals and Expectations 73
    Avoidance 74
    Negative Self-Evaluation 75
Shyness in Children and Adolescents 76
    Children 76
    Teenagers 79
How to Overcome Shyness? 81

Exposure Treatment 81
Cognitive Behavioral Therapy (CBT).................. 85
Learn How to Relax 86

Chapter 5: How to Stop Panic Attacks 89
Treatment 90
    Avoid Stimulants...90
    Practice Breathing..90
    Learn How to Relax 91
    Practice Connection 91
    Physical Exercise.. 93
    Good Sleep 93
What Are the Most Effective Treatments for Panic Disorder? 95
    Cognitive Behavioral Therapy (CBT).................. 95
    Exposure 95
    Medication 96
How to Practice CBT for Panic Attacks 96
What Makes You Vulnerable to Panic Attacks?.. 97
Panic Attacks in Children and Adolescents 99
Panic Attacks in Women 100
Workbook: Panic Attack CBT Worksheets............ 102

Chapter 6: How to Build Your Self-Esteem and Self Confidence...105
The Root of Low Self-Esteem 107
    Inner Criticism.. 108
How the Cycle of Low Self-Esteem Works............ 109
How Does SAD Interact With Low Self-Esteem?...110
    Self-Fulfilling Prophecy 111

How to Improve Self-Esteem With SAD.................112
Cognitive-Behavioral Therapy...........................112
Cognitive Restructuring.....................................112
Exposure Exercises for Self-Esteem..................113

Chapter 7: How to Overcome Social Anxiety and Change Your Life 117
How to Plan Exposure..118
Identify the Problem...119
Prevent Safety Behaviors.................................119
Design Exposures 120
Relaxation Training..121
Learning to Change Anxiety-Provoking Thoughts and Expectations..................................122
How to Prepare for Exposure............................... 124
Create an Exposure Ladder 124
Start From the Bottom.....................................125
Confront Feared Social Situations and Feelings... 126
Practice Confident Body Language 126
Don't Avoid Social Situations 128
Track Your Interactions................................... 128
Find Confident Role Models............................ 129
Resort to Mindfulness 129
Socialize as Often as You Can.......................... 130
Initiate Interactions and Social Events 131
Express Yourself 131
Learn How to Self-Entertain 131
Workbook: Exposure Ladder Ideas 132

Chapter 8: Treatment for Social Anxiety Disorder 135
Why is Social Skills Training Important? 136

Anger Processing 136
Reduce Rumination and Re-evaluation 137
Regain Rational Evaluation............................... 138
Improved Social Skills 142
CBT Treatment Model for Social Anxiety 143
Set Goals... 143
Modify Attention... 144
Improve Self-Image 145
Exposure Treatment... 146
Exposure Tests...147
Mindfulness Treatments for SAD 149
Mindfulness Meditation 150

Chapter 9: Maintaining Your Improvement and Planning for the Future .. 153
How to Maintain Your Improvement 153
Lapse 154
Relapse.. 154
Plan Future Challenges and Improvements 156
Learn From Relapse...157
List Triggers 158
Keep Learning... 159

Conclusion 163

References 167

Introduction

The book in front of you provides a practical solution to your problem with social anxiety. More than a collection of lessons learned through the years of extensive research, it's the result of extensive work done to help one of my dearest family members recover from this disorder. The struggle to help someone I love put me on the path of mental illness exploration and discovering ways to help others. It was a personal experience that changed how I look at my life and the well-being of those around me.

My younger sister, whose experience inspired me to study the condition and eventually share my knowledge with the world, grew up as a quiet, calm, and an all around low maintenance child. As a kid, my sister was obedient and seemingly withdrawn. She very rarely asked for attention. At first, we thought she was just shy. After all, she was developing normally, making friends, and doing just fine at school.

However, when my sister's shyness grew into a full-blown fear of visiting places like playgrounds, and later restaurants and cinemas, my family started to consider the possibility that something wasn't right. Still, we assigned the symptoms to her peculiar personality. We thought of her as an introvert, a loner, and someone who just liked to keep to herself. As there wasn't any obvious explanation for her irrational fears, and there weren't any other behaviors that would signal a mental disorder, we made peace with the fact that "she is the way she is." We loved her for that and tried to help her anyway we could.

While I was unable to help my sister overcome her symptoms, I was well aware of the fact that she was unhappy. Making friends and going out was difficult for her. She chose to stay at home even though she would get invitations to go to parties, and she was getting more than enough date invitations. She pretended she wasn't interested in the events, but I could tell that the truth was she, in fact, was just uncomfortable around other people. Still, I didn't have enough knowledge to name her symptoms for what they were.

It wasn't before going to college and studying mental illnesses that I came across the term social anxiety disorder (SAD). When I started studying this topic, I was, for the first time, able to pinpoint what was wrong with my sister. As I learned about the symptoms and how her disorder developed in childhood, I was finally able to understand what was going on inside my sister's mind. I contacted her and suggested she saw a therapist. With the help of an expert, my sister soon started getting better. Now, she lives a full life. She's no longer afraid of speaking in front of people, and she enjoys making friends. She gladly goes out with her friends and visits clubs, parties, and restaurants.

I, on the other hand, witnessed the drastic difference that therapy made for my sister. I saw a transformation beyond what I believed was possible. I decided not to keep the knowledge to myself, and to compile a clear and comprehensive book for anyone experiencing similar symptoms to find their way around it.

You see, if you're realizing that you or someone you care about has social anxiety, you may not know where to start. Well, I was in your shoes. I know what you don't yet understand about this illness, what needs to be said, and how it needs to be said for you to do it the right way. As someone who observed a person with SAD growing up, I know exactly what the disorder is and how the definition you'll find in books looks in real life.

I have created a reference guide that will help overcome shyness, improve self-confidence, and eliminate panic attacks. Here you will find science-based knowledge that resulted from the years of extensive research on social anxiety. From my personal experience, I included specific sections devoted to teenagers, women, and children.

While other authors make their work based on the experience with patients, I wrote mine based on the experience with helping someone I love. This makes a world of difference. My goal wasn't to get a person from point A to point B. This person wasn't a patient to me; it was someone who had an urgent need to overcome their limitations. It was someone I watched suffer and never lived up to their potential due to fear.

I began to understand what the highest priorities and most important actions that one with social anxiety must take to live a better life. This book will provide the exact instructions to follow, from chapter to chapter, along with a workbook, for anyone with SAD to start recovering NOW.

I can say with full certainty, that by the time you finish reading this book, you will understand what is happening inside your mind and what you need to do to get better. With each chapter, you will learn something about yourself, and what you need to do to alleviate your symptoms.

This book will guide you through understanding social anxiety, from its definitions, types, and mechanisms, to complex ways in which cognitive interactions with the emotional and physiological reflect a person's most profound fears. This book will help you identify the real problem and resolve many misconceptions about social anxiety disorder. Moreover, it will present you with a list of tasks that you can perform to unveil the thoughts that lie beneath distressing symptoms.

This book will provide a unique solution to your problem with social anxiety as these pages contain a self-help manual that will help you plan and execute your recovery. You will learn to evaluate your own social anxiety or help someone who is struggling to understand the severity of their problem. With this understanding, you will be able to set recovery goals and create a plan for daily exercises and exposure therapy so that you can start conquering your fears. After reading this book, you will be better equipped to plan recovery from SAD. With this book alongside a therapist, you will embark on a path of overcoming your greatest fears and embracing your true, authentic self. You will learn how to:

- Overcome constant fear and worry

- Set yourself free from self-criticism, self-doubt, anxiety, and shyness

- Learn how to increase self-esteem by identifying your strengths

- Learn how to be proud of yourself

- Conquer your fear of rejection and start enjoying quality relationships, meeting new people, dating, and advancing your career

- Learn social skills that will enable you to meet other people without fear and anxiety

- Start forming fulfilling relationships, whether they are friendly or romantic

Social anxiety is keeping you in a state of constant fear and causing stress that is often too much to handle. If you are having trouble with small talk or making eye contact, you must read this book now and start learning before your life starts falling apart. There's no need for you to suffer anymore! The sooner you start, the sooner you learn how to overcome these obstacles. This book will help you overcome a feeling of inadequacy and self-imposed limitations to finally be able to enjoy life, make friends, advance and work, and, more importantly, love yourself and others beyond boundaries.

Chapter 1: What is Social Anxiety?

Despite being aware of severe symptoms, I was oblivious to my sister's disorder for a very long time. What I did know was that she was coping with difficult symptoms that were keeping her from living her best life. Learning the basics of social anxiety helped me understand her better, as I believe it will help you see yourself clearly. An in-depth explanation of the condition is useful to evaluate the severity of the symptoms and design the right treatment. In this chapter, you'll learn more about what social anxiety disorder is, and what lies behind the confusing symptoms and mixed feelings you experience in social situations.

Do You Have Social Anxiety Disorder?

Are you simply shy and insecure, or do you have a disorder? Social anxiety disorder is often confused with social anxiety, generalized anxiety, and panic disorder. It's important to understand that having social anxiety isn't the same as having a social anxiety disorder. Social anxiety is a fear of social interaction, but it doesn't necessarily have to be a disorder. Some people experience social anxiety only in certain situations or circumstances (Antony & Swinson, 2000). My sister, along with the majority of people with SAD, fear situations such as:

- Having to speak in front of others unprepared

- Being the center of attention when they're feeling their best

If the fear isn't constant, but rather a result of temporary circumstances, it's too soon to call it a disorder. However, considering that the social anxiety disorder relates to more profound personal issues, you can't exclude the possibility that it will develop if these instances become a pattern.

Is Social Anxiety a Mental Disorder?

Social anxiety disorder is a form of anxiety in which a person is profoundly afraid of others' judgment. If you have a social anxiety disorder, you are worried you'll say or do something to embarrass and humiliate yourself. This fear causes you to isolate yourself, dread social situations, avoid meeting new people, and feel uncomfortable interacting with those who you don't know very well.

The term "disorder" is used when the symptoms become so severe as to interfere with normal life and compromise daily activities, work, and relationships. Simply put, social anxiety can be called a "disorder" when it starts to affect your life significantly. However, the measure of this effect isn't the same for every person. To be diagnosed, you will need an assessment by a psychologist or a psychiatrist, who will carefully examine your symptoms, circumstances, and thinking patterns before they provide a diagnosis. Nowadays, the terms "social anxiety" and "social phobia" are used interchangeably. However, not all experts support this use of terminology. Many prefer using different terms, as they believe that social anxiety is in fact different from social phobia. According to these experts, if untreated, social anxiety may develop into a more severe form or a phobia.

People with social anxiety can be seen as shy, quiet, withdrawn, unfriendly, inhibited, or nervous. You, as well as my sister, my family, and I might be prone to mistake the symptoms for introversion or character quirks. This is not unusual but can prolong suffering and isolation. While people with social anxiety want to form relationships, the fear of judgment holds them back. These fears persist, regardless of the awareness that they're irrational.

Social anxiety disorder is often confused with panic disorder. Social anxiety doesn't induce panic attacks but may cause anxiety attacks. And with anxiety attacks, people don't feel like they are having a medical problem, as they do with panic attacks. While those with panic disorder may feel they need to go to an emergency room because there is something wrong with their body, those with social anxiety know they are overcome with intense fear.

Is Social Anxiety a Mental Disease?

Social anxiety disorder falls under the umbrella of mental illnesses called *anxiety disorders*. However, the criteria for social anxiety disorder are a bit unclear, and having the symptoms doesn't mean you have the disorder. This is one of the main reasons why you shouldn't self-diagnose, but leave the assessment to experts. However, experiencing symptoms that are interfering with your daily life does mean that you should look for the right treatment. While most people face social anxiety on some occasions, people with social anxiety disorder experience the symptoms more intensely, more frequently, and in a greater number of situations than people who don't. With that in mind, here is the criteria for a SAD diagnosis:

- Persistent, intense fear of one or more social situations. This fear is related to anxiety about being judged and scrutinized, doing something humiliating and embarrassing oneself.

- The fears that interfere with normal life. For example, if you have a fear of public speaking, but you are otherwise comfortable speaking to others, then perhaps you don't have a social anxiety disorder. On the other hand, if you have a fear of speaking in front of a small group of people, you may meet the criteria.

- A persistent fear of social and performance situations with exposure to unfamiliar people and being under scrutiny

- Exposure to fearful situations provokes anxiety that can lead to an anxiety attack.

- Recognition that the fear is unreasonable.

- The social situations that trigger the fears are either avoided or endured with intense distress.

- The condition interferes with social activities, and relationships.

- The symptoms can't be attributed to other physiological effects or mental disorders.

- Fear of performance is unrelated to any existing mental disorders.

Social anxiety often relates to other mental problems, like eating disorders, obsessive-compulsive disorder, depression, and others. In these cases, social anxiety can be a part of other, more complex issues. However, just because you have insecurities, self-image, or self-esteem issues, that doesn't mean you have a social anxiety disorder. The best way to find out is to see a therapist or psychiatrist and do an assessment.

How Common is Social Anxiety?

When I started reading into social anxiety, I was surprised at how common it was. Social anxiety is considered to be one of the most common mental problems after phobias, alcoholism, and depression. While the exact number of prevalence of social anxiety hasn't been agreed on, I learned that the same struggles my sister went through struck around 12% of the general population.

Does Social Anxiety Develop in Early Childhood?

I recall my sister being, in a way, different, since she was an infant. She was calmer, more withdrawn, and less interested in exploration and activities. While that might make a parent's life a whole lot easier, it can also be a sign of mental issues. Many studies done on children and adults confirmed that social anxiety disorder most often forms in childhood, before adolescence. While people can overcome social anxiety by their adult years, they are still at higher risk. Some recall having a traumatic experience that triggered anxiety, such as bullying, teasing, or a drastic change of the environment. A majority of adults who participated in studies remember feeling shy and being withdrawn since early childhood. The level of anxiety tends to increase gradually until fearing others' judgment starts to become distressing.

Social anxiety mainly develops in the late teenage years, but it can start in early childhood. Throughout my research, I have discovered that the greatest chance of developing SAD is for those with a family history of the disorder. That made sense to me, as there are a few of my family members who appear to be extremely moody and withdrawn, almost completely detached from society. Within this group, those who have an inhibited temperament in childhood, and appear to be shy, have an increased risk of developing this disorder by their teens. The inhibited temperament is also associated with overly critical and overprotective parenting, but it remains unclear to what degree the parenting style affects the disorder.

Researchers also found that behavioral inhibition in early childhood poses a significant risk factor for social anxiety during middle childhood. It was also the exact trait that stood out in my sister's behavior, and it stands out in many other children with SAD. Behavioral inhibition is a natural, physiological tendency towards shyness, caution, and wariness in unfamiliar settings. The cause of this tendency is in the child's amygdala, the part of the brain that regulates fear. In inhibited children, the amygdala is sensitive, which means that they are overall more prone to fear. At the age of six, behavioral inhibition can indicate future social anxiety in those whose parents suffer from the same disorder. The connections were also found between the behavioral inhibitions in toddlers, the increased generalized social stress in early adolescence, the development of social phobia in high school, as well as social anxiety in adulthood. However, the majority of inhibited children did not develop a social anxiety disorder.

Behavior inhibition mainly associates with increased risk from future social anxiety. Mainly, people with social anxiety fail to recognize the symptoms because they last from a very early age. If you suspect social anxiety, the symptoms may have been with you forever, and you don't recall the time in your life when you felt different. This isn't unusual. Much like my sister, most people seek help after they've been experiencing symptoms for 10 to 20 years.

Social Anxiety in Children

While children and teenagers can be diagnosed with social anxiety disorder, they're more likely to have a generalized form of anxiety. When it comes to children, their symptoms depend on age, but they are always intense and consistent. They include:

- Fear of meeting new people and seeing new items

- Being more irritable and crying more often than other children

- Being quiet and reluctant to speak

- Being prone to "freezing"

- Being "clingy" or fearing to separate from their caregiver

- Fear of reading aloud, talking to others, and performing activities in front of others

- Worrying about others' opinions

- Refusing to partake in performance activities

- Lacking friends or having difficulty maintaining friendships

Anger Problems as an Indicator of SAD

Researchers found a significant connection between problems with anger management and the development of social anxiety in both adults and children. Scientists are still examining this connection, but you can conclude that having social anxiety also means having problems with expressing rage.

Paternal Role in Developing SAD

The research found that fathers have a great impact on the development of social fears and competence. However, the exact impact of family members on the development of social anxiety is yet to be confirmed or explored. If you have a history of problematic relationships with a paternal figure, it is possible that you haven't learned how to manage your fears, which could be the reason why you have a hard time coping with them.

Future Risk of Depression for Children with SAD

Social anxiety in childhood and adolescence links to the future development of depression. Those who experience social anxiety disorder and depression in early childhood and adolescence have a greater chance of having these disorders in adult life. Children who have social anxiety tend to lack friendships and are more likely to develop self-esteem issues because of it. This is why it's considered one of the main reasons for depression and social anxiety to be so closely connected. However, research shows that the younger children are, the easier it is to treat social anxiety. Adolescents and pre-teens are more challenging, which is why early detection is very important.

Severe Fear, Anxiety and Rumination in Adulthood

Fear is one of the basic human emotions. It is run and controlled by the part of your brain in charge of the most primitive physiological responses, called the limbic system. This system causes your mind and body to activate the "fight or flight" response, designed to save a primitive human from imminent danger. While fear is a response to a present threat, anxiety is oriented towards a future threat that can't be prevented or stopped. In other words, when you're anxious, you feel a sense of danger, and you feel like there's nothing you can do to stop it. You fear negative events coming your way that are beyond your control, and you feel defenseless.

Anxiety goes hand-in-hand with rumination, which is the habit of obsessively thinking about unpleasant scenarios and picturing situations that can occur. This puts you in a state of constant worry, which combines with physical symptoms like pain, headaches, muscle tightness, and increased pulse.

Severe anxiety can cause a lot of emotional pain and interfere with one's quality of life and performance. However, that doesn't mean fear is always harmful. To a certain degree, it helps you act responsibly and take good care of yourself, as you're aware of risks that might come from certain behaviors. To a certain degree, anxiety helps you protect yourself from threats and meet the challenges of daily life prepared.

Anxiety and fear are all normal emotions that everyone faces. Typically, they decrease with time — however, people with SAD face chronic physiological responses that intervene in their daily life. They have the purpose of keeping you prepared for future events and are helping you protect yourself from threats. Getting rid of anxiety and fear ultimately shouldn't be your goal; you should aim to reduce the responses so that they don't interfere with your life.

Gender Differences

Men and women's social anxiety is mainly similar, with a few differences. While the research found that SAD is more prevalent in women than in men, these differences can be attributed to the fact that men are less likely to admit feeling anxious. It can also be explained by the fact that women are expected to be more socially active. It was also recorded that men tend to underestimate their fear.

There are also some differences in situations that trigger social anxiety when it comes to gender:

- Men tend to fear to return items to stores and using public restrooms more than women

- Women, on the other hand, tend to be more afraid of public speaking, talking to authority figures, being the center of attention, or disagreeing with others

Causes of Social Anxiety

What causes social anxiety? The answer to this question is complicated, as the disorder results from simultaneous influences of multiple factors:

Genetic Causes

Social anxiety disorder is considered to have a genetic background. Those whose parents had a history of social anxiety disorder are about 30 to 40% more likely to develop the condition. However, determining how genes can cause the disorder and how much is caused by environmental influences and parenting is challenging.

Genetic Aberration

Scientific research proves that a gene called SLCA 4, which is involved in the transport of serotonin, a neurotransmitter that helps stabilize mood and calm down the nerves, may have a lot to do with developing natural tendencies for SAD. Aberrations of this gene are linked to social anxiety, and it's considered that they can pass from parents to children. The imbalance of serotonin has been linked to many symptoms of social anxiety.

The Hyperactive Amygdala and Prefrontal Cortex

It has been determined that those with social anxiety disorder have a hyperactive amygdala, which is responsible for the responses of the body to perceived threats. The activity of the amygdala is amplified by the prefrontal cortex, which is another abnormality discovered in those with SAD. The prefrontal cortex is normally in charge of calming down, but in those with social anxiety, it stimulates the amygdala activity.

Parenting and Early Childhood

Early childhood and parenting styles can also be a cause of social anxiety disorder. Parents can increase the chance of a child developing SAD when they are overly critical, less attentive, over-controlling, and overly concerned with the opinions of others. When parents are too critical and overprotective of the child, they tend to create a tense environment in which the child never feels completely safe and accepted.

Overprotective parents hover over their children, disallowing the child to learn through their own experiences and mistakes. This kind of parent is upset whenever the child falls, cries, or faces any unpleasantness. They don't allow the child to become resilient to disturbance and pain or learn how to process and resolve conflict and negative feelings. These parents assume the role of a protector, and the child grows up feeling incompetent to solve problems and face difficulties on their own. The child's problem-solving and communication skills can become impaired; their coordination and motor skills develop slower. In teens and adult years, a person becomes socially anxious as they don't believe in their ability to manage and solve problems on their own.

Critical parents can damage a child's self-esteem in many ways. They consistently point out the child's "flaws," pointing out every error and imperfection. These parents highlight the child's weakness but completely ignore or deny their strengths and good sides. As a result, a child develops a negative self-image. Social anxiety happens as a result of the profoundly negative self-image and unconscious beliefs in one's inadequacy and unworthiness. When a parent is overly concerned by the opinions of others, they can transfer this to the child, and the child starts feeling like they'll be judged harshly regardless of what they do.

These influences can shape the child's self-image and how they see the world. When overly controlling parents raise children, they can become less trusting of others and more fearful, which can negatively impact their self-confidence. Social anxiety disorder usually starts developing during the early teenage years and becomes chronic.

Unsafe Environment

The environmental influences can also contribute to developing a social anxiety disorder. Environmental impacts that can cause social anxiety include:

- Different forms of trauma, such as emotional, sexual, or physical

- Teasing and bullying

- Living in a violent, unstable environment

- Desertion, or death of close ones

- Maternal stress

These influences can reinforce the belief that people shouldn't be trusted, and the world is scary and unpredictable. This is especially harmful to children, who can feel profoundly hurt by their closest ones. In adulthood, this can lead to developing perfectionism. Perfectionism is also a trait learned in early childhood. Being a perfectionist means that you have a tendency to set unrealistically high standards for yourself. These standards are impossible to meet and always lead to self-criticism, as everything can always be done better.

Symptoms of Social Anxiety

If you think about shyness, you think about a quiet person, someone who finds it hard to open up. Someone whose cheeks blush when you're talking to them, avoiding eye contact, and lowering their eyes. However, social anxiety isn't at all sweet, and the person feels anything but good in this situation. Social anxiety is difficult to live with, as it includes numerous difficult symptoms, such as:

- Intense fear or panic
- Severe sweating
- Heart racing
- Trembling
- And others

However, these symptoms are only superficial signs of more serious underlying problems. The reason why social situations are triggering to many is that they awaken profound self-defeating thoughts and beliefs that cause severe negative self-criticism. This mechanism triggers due to damaged self-esteem but originates from the negative, irrational core beliefs about oneself and the world. On an elementary level, social anxiety happens because a person feels profoundly inadequate and unlikeable, and they fear that they'll be seen as dull, stupid, etc.

Fear of embarrassment is intense with SAD, mainly in the form of the general fear of being judged negatively. Those with social anxiety fear that people will notice their symptoms, and that fear itself is often enough for them to avoid social situations.

What Triggers Social Anxiety?

I clearly remember my sister becoming red in her face whenever she had to introduce herself to someone. I also remember her dodging family events whenever she could, and she never looked people in the eyes. On the outside, it almost looked like she thought too highly of herself. If I didn't know her better, I'd think of her as an unlikeable, arrogant person. What I didn't understand was that all of these were symptoms of social anxiety, and they were being triggered in situations in which she was the center of attention. These are called performance situations. There are many examples, but the most common include:

- Engaging in conversations

- Talking to authority figures

- Attending social events

- Interacting with new people

- Being interviewed for a job

- Saying "no"

- Confrontation

- Making eye contact

Performance situations that often trigger SAD include:

- Speaking in public

- Participating in social activities

- Being watched while you perform

Intense physiological responses to these situations may extend to even mundane daily activities, like returning an item to a store, using public restrooms, asking for assistance or directions, making a mistake in public, or walking down the street. The simple act of introducing yourself can also trigger symptoms.

Social anxiety means feeling nervous and uncomfortable in social situations. This usually happens because you fear being judged or doing something to embarrass yourself. You are afraid of making a bad impression. All of these fears actually relate to the fear of criticism. People react differently in social situations, and some may be more comfortable in business settings and less in person, while for others, it's the other way around. The intensity of the symptoms and the range of situations that trigger anxiety vary in different people. For some, the fear is easy to manage, while others are completely overpowered by it and find it hard to function in society. People with social anxiety suffer profoundly because of their isolation. While you may be yearning to relax, connect, and get to know new people, your withdrawn exterior may cause people to think of you as arrogant or unfriendly.

Although social anxiety is hard to cope with, it is highly treatable. As you've learned in this chapter, the reason why you feel such intense, unexplainable fear and shame is more profound than simple shyness. In the following chapter, you'll learn more about how social anxiety is affecting your life. With this knowledge, it will be easier for you to understand what are your biggest triggers, and which areas of social functioning you want to focus on.

SAD Symptoms Checklist

- Feeling uncomfortable or afraid to speak with authority figures (e.g., boss, teacher)

- Feeling embarrassed because you think that other people can see that you are blushing

- Being afraid that other people will notice that you're sweating

- Being afraid of social events

- Avoiding talking to people you don't know very well

- Avoiding going to parties

- Being afraid of talking to strangers

- Avoiding public performance

- Fear of being criticized

- Willingness to do anything to avoid criticism

- Feeling heart palpitations when you're around people, especially new

- Being afraid of doing things when you feel like people are watching you

- Fear of being embarrassed or looking stupid

- Avoiding speaking in front of authority figures

- Worrying that others can notice your fears

- Intense fear and nervousness

- Negative emotional cycles that are automatic

- Negative perceptions and self-evaluations

Chapter 2: Effects of Social Anxiety in Real Life

Even while I was unaware of my sister's condition, I was sure her shyness was ruining her life. Eventually, she started distancing from her friends, going on fewer dates, and spending more and more time watching TV. It no longer looked like she enjoyed anything besides sitting in her room by herself. It wasn't long before she started having problems at work. She was less and less productive as time went by, and we became concerned that she might lose her job. Her friends were calling less frequently, thinking that she's too busy with work to socialize. Meanwhile, my sister was suffering alone. Oblivious to her condition, she didn't understand what was happening to her, but she began to see that her life was falling apart.

Indeed, the damage that this condition can have on your life can be more severe than a mere inconvenience. While you may feel insecure in your abilities, and this insecurity causes many of your symptoms, it is also true that the anxiety does have a harmful impact on your skills and abilities. In return, the damaged capacities only enhance negative self-image, further worsening the symptoms. Because the effects of avoidance damage make you feel bad about yourself and further keep you from being happy and satisfied, social anxiety increases the risk of substance abuse, depression, or even suicide attempts.

Social anxiety can disrupt your daily life, limit work efficiency, and reduce self-esteem. In relationships, being socially anxious can cause feelings of powerlessness, shame, and loneliness. You might fear that others will negatively judge you or they are evaluating your every move. Always being aware of your perceived flaws can cause you to feel embarrassed without a particular reason or a strategy to resolve the feelings.

- You imagine yourself saying or doing something inappropriate or unintelligent

- You think that tiny imperfections in your appearance are visible and draw attention

- You make assumptions that people think you are boring, incompetent, or otherwise inadequate

In addition, the constant fear of scrutiny and negative judgment gets in the way of learning and education. You may delay finishing and turning in school assignments because the high standards you've set for yourself are difficult or impossible to achieve. Constant worry regarding schoolwork and exams doesn't have to be intense to cause harm. It is enough for it to be ever-present, even in lower intensity, to drain mental and physical energy. As a result, you may get tired faster than your peers while learning, which takes a toll on your grades and overall school achievement. Social anxiety disorder has been proven to have harmful effects on all aspects of life, which is why it's critically important for you to understand that:

- Failing to address symptoms will harm your life on all levels

- The reduction of quality of life and lower achievement only worsen your self-image and symptoms

On the other hand, measuring the impact that social anxiety has on your life and committing to getting will produce more success. This success will, in return, improve your confidence, increasing your chances of recovery. The following sections will review the effects of social anxiety on different areas of your life.

How Does Social Anxiety Affect Your Life?

Worrying about others' opinions and fearing negative judgment are making it difficult to go through job interviews, get jobs, and maintain professional careers. Overall, social anxiety prevents people, and possibly you, from living a healthy life. Here's how being socially anxious affects different areas of your life (Barrera & Norton, 2009):

Everyday Interactions

Socially anxiety can make daily interactions appear difficult or even impossible.

- Avoiding shopping in stores when they are crowded

- Fearing phone calls, and feeling anxious about how you'll sound over the phone

- Worrying about how another person will react to what you're saying

- Avoiding eating or working in public

All of these limitations can take a toll on your activities, diet, health, and social life.

Physical Health

Avoiding social situations where you feel like your appearance will be judged can keep you from being active, getting enough fresh air, and getting exercise. Avoiding exercise or going to the gym is common for those who worry that others will notice their flaws. Such examples as:

- You avoid going out, which affects your relationships, health, and mood

- You're not getting food, medication, and other necessities on time

- You're not as active as you should be, which affects your energy and fitness levels

Family Life

We like to think our families are safe environments. However, if you have social anxiety, even family gatherings can be stressful. Unique dynamics can further complicate the fear of familial judgment. Familial relationships can be complex, and hardly anyone has a family without at least one issue. With social anxiety, these issues become enhanced due to an increased fear of judgment and oversensitivity to criticism. Instead of enjoying a casual lunch with your relatives, you might fear that they are comparing you with other, seemingly more successful relatives. You might fear that everyone in the room knows your "embarrassing" secrets and that they are secretly judging, pitying, or mocking you.

During family gatherings, social anxiety symptoms can be triggered in specific situations or with specific family members. People might feel judged by some family members, but feel closer and safer with others.

Examples

- Avoiding familial gatherings because you feel nervous and anxious around certain relatives

- Avoiding personal topics because you fear your family will judge your every word or action

- Avoiding family members who bring up issues that are sensitive because the physical symptoms are hard to bear (e.g., Your father gives you a hard time for being unemployed, or a mother who constantly asks about your marriage plans.)

- Being on-edge and prone to arguments when triggered by vague remarks (when your mother asks, *"Are you going to finish that?"* and in your mind, it comes off as a comment on your weight)

- Over-reacting when someone criticizes your parenting or comments on your work, finances, or romantic life

Family issues are common even without social anxiety. As it happens, families are the social groups that tend to challenge self-image and self-esteem the most. As a result, they trigger profound beliefs of inadequacy, self-critical thoughts, and feelings of shame, which all result in overwhelming physical symptoms.

Personal Relationships

The effects of constantly feeling inadequate and expecting bad judgment by others can interfere with all aspects of relationships, from those with strangers to friends, and even romantic relationships. Social interactions, such as small talk, can seem difficult. In these circumstances, even casual conversations might seem impossible. With some, the anxiety may increase as the relationship progresses and they start to feel the negativity. Examples of this behavior are:

- Avoiding going out and meeting your friends

- Not returning calls

- Canceling arrangements

- Feeling inadequate and fearing that a friend or a romantic partner is going to stop loving you once they discover who you truly are

- Ending relationships once they start to become close

- Unwillingness to spend time with friends

- Reluctance to be assertive, and state your opinion

Romantic

People with social anxiety tend to withhold expressions of negative emotions, which hurts their relationships. The more people feel free to communicate negative emotions in practical ways, the better chance of successful romantic relationships. For example:

- Believing that withholding emotions lead to a better quality relationship. This becomes a strategy of maintaining closeness in a relationship that has negative consequences in the long run

- Withholding opinions, beliefs, and intentions due to fear of rejection

- Accepting to lose authenticity if it will preserve the relationship. This has both social, and relationship affects

- Believing that it is enough that the relationship exists so that you feel close to the other person, regardless of the quality of the relationship

- Acting passive and submissive to avoid conflicts

Research suggests that people who feel that their relationship is close enough for expressing negative emotions feel safer and better supported in these relationships. However, there is an irony in the need to express feelings in relationships and the loss of authenticity that socially anxious people tend to do. Holding in feelings can hurt well-being and psychological health. Typically, expressing and sharing feelings leads to better social support and forming intimate relationships, whether they are romantic or friendly.

Friendships

Studies have found that those with social anxiety disorder mainly experience a lack of social life and fun activities. These effects were most severe when it came to social networking (extreme worry about performance in communication with others) and romantic relationships. When it comes to friendships, studies found that those with a social anxiety disorder had fewer friends than they would like.

Work

Avoiding social situations harms personal and professional relationships, and leads to poor social skills, oversensitivity to criticism, depression, and low self-esteem. Severe social anxiety can interfere with workplace performance. It might affect your choice of jobs and your performance at work. People with social anxiety may turn down a promotion or drop out of college due to the severity of symptoms. Unwillingness to speak in front of people causes slower progress work. You might be afraid of speaking to coworkers or avoid talking to them overall. Some even find it hard to go to work and become unemployed. On the other hand, avoiding coworkers and answering questions with only a few simple words can cause you to be seen as a snob or an arrogant.

Social anxiety disorder is linked to reduced productivity as well as short-term and long-term work disability. On average, people with anxiety lose about 4.6 days per month and 18.1 per three months, as well as around five days due to lost productivity. They have a higher risk of being absent from work for at least two weeks. Sleep problems get in the way of productivity. Progress at work is an important part of healing. Here are a couple of things people with SAD struggle with at work:

- Schedules and deadlines
- Planning
- Organization
- Skill building
- Projects that involve public speaking
- Communication

Business Meetings

Participating in business meetings can be very difficult for anyone who fears to be the center of attention. Meetings require active participation in terms of both speaking and listening. Fear of judgment can cause people to refrain from stating their opinions, as they tend to avoid confrontation. Avoiding confrontation results from the fear of looking foolish and saying the wrong thing or not enough.

People with social anxiety fear that they will be negatively evaluated and judged harshly by others.

While your colleagues have no problem speaking up and defending their suggestions, even if they know they're wrong, you might stay silent even if you know you're right. Somewhere, in the back of your head, there's a possibility that you are actually wrong and you'll make a fool out of yourself if you say something. While you may know that your fears are irrational, they are so severe that you decide to stay quiet just so that you don't have to face them.

Physical signs, on their own, can make work meetings harder. Research shows that people with social anxiety think that their symptoms are more visible than they actually are. While no one notices your sweating and nervousness, you might avoid showing up or actively participating in preventing the risk of others witnessing your symptoms.

Depression and Social Anxiety

It is considered that social anxiety disorder is the most common form of anxiety in those with a history of depression. However, which of these disorders leads to another is yet to be proven. Some explanations relate to the fact that there are common genetic factors for developing both conditions. Social anxiety, in combination with avoidance, contributes to social isolation and demoralization, which are all risk factors for depression.

Social anxiety disorder is associated with an increased risk of developing depressive disorders. The social anxiety disorder, in combination with depression, worsens the prognosis. When compared to those who have a depressive disorder without social anxiety, those with social anxiety have increased chances of recurrent depression, and their depressive symptoms are more persistent.

Eating Disorders

There is also a strong connection between social anxiety disorders and eating disorders. However, it hasn't been determined which aspects of social anxiety contribute to developing eating disorders. The assumption is that the presence of fear of negative judgment and the vulnerabilities that come with having social anxiety increases a person's risk of developing eating disorders. Some of the aspects of social anxiety that might affect eating disorders include:

- Fear of social interaction

- Fear of negative judgment being anxious about their social appearance

- The fear of positive judgment

Being self-aware of one's appearance links to dissatisfaction with one's own body, increasing concerns about shape and weight. In addition, fear of negative judgment creates a drive for restraint from food. Being anxious about one's body image increases risks from eating disorders — the higher the anxiety, the greater the awareness of the physical appearance. As a result, restraint from eating can occur, and the risks of developing eating disorders increase.

Being unsatisfied with one's own body is one of the biggest risks for developing eating disorders. Those who are anxious about their social and physical appearance and fear negative judgment are highly vulnerable to developing an eating disorder. Anxiety over the social appearance and fear of negative judgment leads to greater concerns about weight and shape. There is also a connection with dissatisfaction with one's own body and the development of bulimia. Those with greater appearance anxiety have a greater risk of developing *bulimia nervosa*, while those with fear of negative judgment tend to have a greater risk of developing *anorexia nervosa*.

Social Anxiety and Autism

The lack of social skills is often associated with autism. Increased social anxiety was found both in those with social anxiety disorder and those with autism. Both groups of people tend to struggle with social skills. Some symptoms are common for autism and social anxiety, such as problems with attention and the lack of social skills. It was found that both groups have issues with flexibility and the ability to plan. Genetic factors are also connected to social anxiety and those who have autism. However, it can't be confirmed that everyone who has autism also suffers from social anxiety and vice versa. While there are some similarities, these are two completely different disorders. In addition, the treatments that are effective in treating autism aren't effective in treating social anxiety. One of the main differences between the two is in the levels of anxiety. Intense anxiety is the main characteristic of SAD, but not autism.

Types of Phobias

If your social anxiety is very severe, you could be wondering whether or not you have a phobia. The term *social phobia* means a multitude of consistent fears that relate to social performance situations and interactions with the possibility of others' scrutiny. As mentioned in the first chapter, while social phobia and social anxiety disorder are now one in the same, many therapists and psychiatrists still use them separately due to subtle differences.

It is estimated that around 30% of the population meets the criteria for diagnosing social phobia at one point in their life. Social phobia may impact one's life and cause many problems in everyday functioning. Problems that most relate to social phobia include test and performance anxiety, which means that the symptoms are triggered in situations in which oneself is in some form, tested.

The rates are also high in alcohol and substance abuse, as well as social isolation. There are also problems with maintaining a career. However, since roughly 40% of the population considers themselves to be shy, it was tough to distinguish this disorder from shyness until recently. Social phobia was considered to be a neglected form of anxiety disorder.

Shyness, Social Phobia, and Avoidant Personality Disorder

A distinction needs to be made between the terms *social phobia, avoidant personality disorder,* and *shyness*. While some researchers consider these to be separate mental disorders, others see them as a continuum from one end of the spectrum when it comes to symptoms of worry of social evaluation. In this case, the hierarchy of disorders goes as follows:

- Shyness is on the lower range of the continuum
- Social phobia meets the medium and higher range
- Avoidant personality disorder, which is the most extreme form

Types of Social Phobia

There are also multiple types of social phobia. Social phobia is often divided into two subtypes;

- **Generalized social phobia** with which people experience fears in the majority of social situations.

- **Restricted social phobia** where symptoms only occur in certain social situations. People with restricted social phobia have specific fears, for example, public speaking.

As I learned more about the different shades of social anxiety, I started to see which of my sister's self-esteem issues were the most severe, and which needed urgent attention. This was when I began to understand how she truly feels when she acts cold and distant, and it helped me figure out how to help her. If you want to help yourself or someone you love recover from social anxiety, make sure to review all the symptoms and go through all the described effects of the condition. This will help you identify the most active issues and triggers. With this knowledge, you'll be able to make a more accurate self-evaluation. Based on that, you'll be able to use the instructions provided in the following chapters with greater confidence and accuracy.

Chapter 3: Getting to Know Your Social Anxiety Disorder

One of the first things I wanted to know when I started studying SAD was how to help my sister cope. I knew the background of her condition, but the theoretical knowledge meant nothing if she was unable to deal with it and improve her life. I started learning more about the disorder. I learned that SAD isn't much like physical diseases, where the same symptoms, laboratory test results, and medicines suit all people. Instead, it is a profoundly personal disorder. You see, every mind is like a universe in its own. Every person has their own, unique experiences, thoughts, and images going through their mind. While different schools of psychology recognize mental structures, thought patterns, and personality traits, how each individual experiences their mental state is unique for every person.

For example, I am an incredibly visual person. To me, everything that shows up in my mind is displayed in some form. Whenever my mind tries to tell me something I am unwilling to hear, it surfaces as a memory, a song, or an image of the situation. While I respected my sister's privacy enough not to ask such questions, I understood that, in order for others to understand their SAD, they must do some mind excavating. This mainly works alongside a therapist. Since they are only able to evaluate the things you communicate, you must look into and track your thoughts, feelings, and sensations. One of the ways to do this is by breaking down your anxious episodes into different aspects, and then analyze how they mutually interact. SAD has a cognitive, emotional, and physical component (Hope, 2003). What does this mean? Let's look at an example of a time you could have felt extremely awkward in a social setting:

Being late to an appointment or a date. The truth is, people arrive late all the time and it is certainly not the end of the world if you do. If you have SAD, chances are, being unable to get somewhere on time causes a lot of tension for you. If this were the case, I would assume you arrive at the location in extreme discomfort. Your heart is racing, you feel stressed, and consider not going in because of your tardiness. So, what happens? In this situation, your mind appears somewhat blurry and chaotic, but three other things are likely happening underneath:

Cognitive: You either consciously or unconsciously think, *"I'm late. I'm always late. This is embarrassing. They think I'm slow, lazy, and incompetent because I am."* You might be aware of some of these thoughts, but others, if too painful to acknowledge, pass so quickly you don't even notice.

Emotional: You feel. Emotions never happen on their own; conscious or unconscious thoughts cause them. On most occasions, people with SAD feel a painful mix of fear and shame. Shame comes from thinking bad about yourself, while fear comes from thinking that everyone else notices your "flaws" and that something bad will happen as a result of them. You may project this fear to the fear of the situation outcome, but deep down, your fear your own perceived inadequacy.

Physical: This course of mental events causes a physiological reaction. Fear, on its own, sends the blood rushing through your body, increasing your heart rate and making you feel like you want to run and hide. Shame, on the other hand, causes a mix of embarrassment, sadness, or anger that makes your cheeks blush, your throat dry, and your hands to shake. Combine the two, and you get a profoundly painful experience that can range from discomfort to a panic or anxiety attack.

Once I learned this, I started to understand some of my sister's behaviors. For example, she'd be excited about going out with friends. As the time approaches to start getting ready, she starts to procrastinate. Suddenly, her room needs tidying, and she starts to feel tired. She then needs a nap, and a cup of coffee. By the time she heads to the shower, she doesn't have enough time to get ready. She lets her friends know she'll meet them later. But, the later never comes and she just goes to bed. Does this sound familiar? I also noticed her starting to do this with important appointments, exams, and even work. As I was learning about what's going on in her mind, I understood her thinking. In her mind, getting ready meant she'd look at herself in the mirror, overly conscious of perceived flaws. She'd have all these awful thoughts about herself that scared her at first, but later just drained her physically to the point she was unable to leave the house.

I believe something similar is happening to you whenever you're supposed to confront an "awkward" situation. Luckily, there's a great way to break down your anxious episodes so that you can navigate them better. This technique is called *thought record*, and it's a great way to understand how the things you think and feel cause your physical symptoms. It helps you break down the three essential components of SAD and understand what triggers the anxiety. Here's what you need to do to understand your SAD.

Before you start, it's good to recall a situation that made you feel anxious. Pay attention to the following elements (Antony& Swinson, 2000):

Screen your body from top to bottom and detect the physical sensations. This way, you'll reveal how the situation affects your body. The physiological (physical, organic, biological) component of SAD refers to the way you feel when you are anxious. What happens inside your body when you are feeling anxious? The three main symptoms include heart-pounding (palpitations), feeling flush, and shaky hands. In a distressing situation, the first thing you want to do is to track the physical symptoms. Here are some of the possible symptoms:

Head & Neck

- Dizziness
- Headache
- Blurry vision
- Lump in the throat
- Flushing

Chest

- Chest tightness
- Heart racing
- Chest pain
- Smothering feeling

Limbs and Muscles

- Shakiness
- Muscle pains

Overall

- Depersonalization-feeling distant from your own body

If you have four or more of the symptoms, you could be having a panic attack. While the sensation may feel intense, and for some, it feels like an adrenaline rush, it would only last a couple of minutes. After that, the symptoms will subside. Here are a couple of symptoms typical for panic attacks: heart pounding, sweating, choking, heart racing, numbness/tingling, dizziness, flushing, nausea, stomach aches, shortness of breath, trembling/shaking, fear of insanity or dying.

Some of the described symptoms aren't physical but can occur because experiencing it for the first time can feel like a heart attack or a mental breakdown. While this is intense and very scary, the symptoms will alleviate after a couple of minutes. If they don't, or if the attacks persist, that means that you might be having a panic disorder.

With social anxiety, panic attacks happen in social situations or performance situations that make you feel afraid and insecure. You will be worried about how people see your anxiety. On the other hand, with panic disorders, you'll be more worried about the physical symptoms, and their implications to your physical and mental health.

Your SAD shows its face in the sensations it produces, but it begins with thoughts. The cognitive part of SAD consists of the ideas that appear in a triggering situation. While you may not be fully aware of it, certain conditions trigger fast, almost undetectable thoughts inside your mind. But, what makes your thoughts different than everyone else's, and why are they so disturbing?

Self-Criticism. The reason why your thoughts assume the lead role in SAD is because they revolve around negative self-judgment. Now is the time to realize one of the biggest truths about SAD: your own harsh, negative self-judgment triggers the fear of others' negative judgment. You fear certain situations because they alarm the already-existing beliefs, that are always with you, albeit unconsciously.

Negative core beliefs. In the earlier example of being late, the thought process started with *"They'll think,"* which is a display of your fear of judgment. It ended, however, with the thought *"I am."* This thought reflects how you feel about yourself. What leads to this is a belief. In a person's mental structure, beliefs create the very basics of your mentality and your personality. Core beliefs relate to the underlying attitudes about the world, life, people, and yourself. They're created in early infancy, based on the ways you were treated by your caregivers, but also your experiences. Whatever happened during your youngest years, installed negative beliefs about yourself. Parents and caregivers are most often blamed for the creation of negative core beliefs during early childhood, but the situation isn't black and white. It is essential to clarify so you don't assume the way you are today means you had a rough childhood or a non-loving family.

Childhood trauma can spawn from even a seemingly nice upbringing. Even if certain traumatic events don't seem traumatizing to the level of neglect or abuse, they can still glue to your perception of being. These beliefs, with anxiety, and the most relevant ones being that you are unworthy, incompetent, wrong, or not enough, lie dormant while going about your daily life. However, they unconsciously navigate and guide your behaviors, while the majority of your conscious mind is present, alert, and clueless of what goes on below the surface. However, in social situations, one of those beliefs awakens and creates self-defeating thoughts. This process is intellectual, invisible, and unconscious. But, as you encounter thoughts that scare you, your body starts creating physiological responses.

Thoughts That Trigger Anxiety

To break down your SAD triggers, you'll have to trace the thoughts that activated in the situation. These thoughts revolve around your fear of judgment and scrutiny, and originate from your negative self-judgment and self-afflicted-scrutiny tracing back to negative core beliefs. Due to the nature of SAD, these thoughts are often hidden from your conscious mind. In general, they relate to some of the following:

- *"I'm stupid"*
- *"I'm incompetent"*
- *"I'm unattractive"*
- *"I'm unlikeable"*

The key to managing SAD isn't in treating all thoughts; just those that tend to produce anxious reactions. To do this, you'll have to analyze the last situation in which you recall feeling the symptoms of social anxiety. This means remembering the previous situation where the prospect of a social situation was so challenging that you either avoided the situation or went through it with a great deal of discomfort. One of the simpler ways to trace triggering thoughts is to go back into that moment and try to recall the situation as vividly as possible. Next, you want to note how the situation played out and how it made you feel. Write down everything you remember about a situation. Write down everything you remember about your surroundings, including how it made you feel. Now, focus on your thoughts at the moment. Try to trace some of them and write them down.

Not all thoughts affect you the same way. Some of them were less intense, and some of them more. Your next goal is to trace the most intense thoughts to reveal the so-called *"hot"* thought, which embodies the irrational belief you carry. This thought, compared to others, triggers the most intense feelings and physiological responses. You can rate them on a scale from 1 to 100, or by intensity. Breaking down the last situation you remember will help you understand what thought pattern causes you the most distress. It is important to realize that most people have some degree of these thoughts. It only becomes problematic when these thought patterns have a detrimental impact on your life.

One of the ways to understand the severity of your disorder is to track past experiences and analyze them. The same way you interpreted the last triggering event, you should recall as many from your past as possible and break them down in the same way. This way, you'll manage to notice your overall thought pattern, and discover the most prevalent fears, triggering situations, and self-defeating thoughts.

Now that you can recall the situations, it is time to look into the worst experiences that were similar or associated with what you experience today. Most likely, these experiences go back in childhood and early adolescence. They are very painful for you to remember, but it is probably the best way to understand when your anxiety issues truly began. Think back to the worst situation you can recall that was socially awkward for you, and break it down for yourself. If there are multiple situations, feel free to explore as many as you can. Repeat the process of tracing back your thoughts and feelings in these situations, and rate them. Most likely, you'll notice that the severity and intensity of the feelings those thoughts induced increased over time, which shows you exactly how your illness progressed.

Now that you've looked into the situations that have most likely caused a disorder to develop, it is time to look into the exact thoughts that appeared in these situations. In particular, you should look into the thoughts that seem to have the strongest effect on you. These are exact thoughts that are triggering your fears. Having these thoughts in mind will help you proceed with your treatment, as you'll know which beliefs you want to target and overcome.

Track Behaviors

When you've determined the exact thoughts that are triggering SAD, you should go back and identify the behaviors that the anxiety produces. Most often, these are the so-called *avoidant behaviors* that serve to relieve the tension and protect you from the fears and self-criticism. However, these behaviors don't help you overcome the disorder in the long run. They are only temporarily relieving the symptoms. Other than avoidance, overcompensation and over self-checking are some of the behaviors typically used to cope with SAD.

Avoidant behaviors can include, quite literally, the avoidance of the situation, but they can also include procrastination and other habits that serve to shelter you from emotional hurt.

Overcompensation, on the other hand, means obtaining what you feel like you're lacking. For example, if you're self-conscious, you may pay too much attention to your looks or overspend as a way of upgrading yourself. If you're conscious of your weight, you may overeat as a result of compensating for the lack of satisfaction with your body. This is the reason why overeating is so frequent in obese people. If your SAD affects your relationships, you may compensate by being overly submissive in a relationship, or too eager to please everyone due to fear of rejection.

To track all of these behaviors, write down your activities before, during, and after the triggering situations:

- Are there any common threads or patterns in your behavior?

- If so, how do they impact your life?

- What can you do to stop with these behaviors, and calm yourself down instead?

Social Anxiety in Children and Adolescents

Children and adolescents can suffer from SAD, equally as adults. The same causes that were already mentioned apply to SAD in children. Children can inherit the genetic factors that increase the likelihood of developing this disorder, but environmental influences also play an essential role. While shy children have a slightly higher risk of developing SAD in adult life, that doesn't have to be a rule. Like adults, children can fear negative judgment when it comes to social performance. Children respond immediately to these stressors, displaying intense fear and avoidance. To be diagnosed with SAD, a child's life needs to be significantly impaired by the symptoms.

Adolescents, on the other hand, need to meet the criteria of being able to tell that their feelings and thoughts are irrational. Children and adolescents with SAD have the same symptoms as adults, except that they tend to be more sensitive to criticism, and less assertive. Children with SAD are more prone to angry outbursts and crying, and can be seen as oversensitive by their parents and peers.

When a child has SAD, their friendships and education tend to suffer the most. Children can develop low self-esteem and underachieve at school while adolescents are more prone to avoidant behaviors than aggression.

Workbook: SAD Thought Record Worksheet

Self-evaluation is one of the ways for you to assess the severity of your SAD. Making an evaluation and measuring the severity means you look into the intensity, frequency, and types of situations that trigger the symptoms, and also how they affect your life. There are numerous ways for you to perform a self-evaluation. One of these ways is to use a journal and track your past and present experiences. When journaling, pay attention to write down as many situations as you can remember and continue writing down the situations in the present.

Next, you want to separate thoughts as a category from physical sensations and emotions that these thoughts produce. You can later proceed to scale and rate these thoughts, feelings, and sensations, to pinpoint the typical thinking patterns and typical responses that result in these situations.

Tracking your triggering situations will help you discover not only the nature of your strongest fears but also the areas of your life that are suffering as well. Typically, SAD relates to fear of rejection, which leads to issues in relationships, while the performance-related SAD leads to financial troubles.

Write down as many situations you can think of, and write down all the avoidant behaviors and other coping strategies that you've been using. After that, make a rough assessment of the effects that these behaviors are having on your life. Your self-evaluation should contain the following elements:

Situation

- Describe the physical setting and the environment.
- How did the situation look?
- Who was involved?
- Were you indoors or outdoors?
- If you were inside, how did the room look?
- What happened that caused you to start feeling anxious?

- What did you hear?
- What did you see?

Emotions

- What did you feel after the interaction? Was it fear? Shame? Guilt?

Physical Symptoms

- What physical symptoms did you feel?

Thoughts

- What do you remember thinking during this situation? Write down all of your thoughts.

Behaviors

- What were you doing before the situation?
- What do you remember doing during the situation? Do you remember making any hand gestures, leg movements?
- Do you remember doing any activities to calm yourself down?
- What did you do after the event? How did you calm yourself down? Did you check your phone, or had a drink, or got something to eat?

- Are these behaviors now extending to non-triggering situations?

- How do you think that these situations affected your life?

- How do you think your avoidant behaviors affected your relationships?

- How did these behaviors affect your work?

- How are these behaviors affecting your health?

Here is an example of a self-evaluation form:

Situation (Time and Place)	Emotions	Physical Symptoms	Thoughts	Behaviors

Chapter 4: How to Overcome Shyness

What is shyness? Ever since my sister was little, she was known as shy. It was sweet at first. At age two to five, she was a calm, quiet girl who didn't speak up. While my family appreciated having a child who didn't throw tantrums when she didn't get what she wanted and wasn't interested in talking to strangers, unbeknownst to us, she was in considerable discomfort. Who doesn't love a quiet child? Who doesn't like when their child stays away from strangers and never disobeys, jumps around, or causes mischief in public places? While not all children who fit this profile have social anxiety, it's not without reason that psychologists claim that a healthy child is the one that causes you headaches. We, as a family, learned this soon enough. When my sister's shyness started to keep her away from making friends and doing her best at school, we began to see that shyness is something that can cause great pain. On the outside, it may appear sweet, and a sign of humble, gentle nature. They are the ones who are lonely, yet unable to connect. They are the ones who crave connection, but can't look at you in the eye. When I started studying social anxiety, shyness first came to mind, as it was the most apparent quality I observed and the most distressing. It was also, as I soon learned, quite simple to treat if you're willing to step out of your comfort zone.

It's best to describe shyness as a feeling of inner tension, discomfort, and anxiety that you feel when talking to other people. Shyness is more common than you think. Roughly 80% of people report feeling shy at least at one point in their life, meaning that occasional shyness is nothing to worry about. However, when your symptoms are so severe as to get in the way of successful social interaction, you can think about possibly seeking treatment. Intense feelings of shyness can cause you to avoid situations that trigger feelings, resulting in considerable impairment to the quality of your life. You may lose the ability to enjoy shopping and miss out on important information as you avoid asking questions, whether it's to a teacher, doctor, bank clerk, cashier, or even on a date. Shyness can even keep you from getting the necessary medicine if you're too embarrassed to talk about your condition to a doctor or pharmacist.

Shyness is often present in social anxiety, although not always. Remember, people with SAD can fear certain, specific social situations, but not all. Luckily, it is treatable. In this chapter, you will learn more about the mental and physiological mechanisms behind shyness and the strategies you can use to overcome it.

The biggest damage from being too shy comes from avoidance, a common denominator in all SAD, and anxiety-related disorders. If you create a pattern of avoiding situations that cause shyness, the intensity of the sensations gradually gets worse. You may fear, or altogether avoid the following situations:

- Public speaking, whether it's at school or work

- Public eating and drinking, meaning that you might stop going out to dinners and clubs with friends and family, or even avoid social events overall

- Enjoying entertainment, like dancing, playing sports, and attending concerts

- Making small talk with strangers, meaning that you'll stop meeting new people

- Participating in group conversations

- You may become too fearful of approaching others

What Makes You Shy?

A shy person is also anxious, without a doubt. You can also assume they're insecure, sure enough, and they may not like themselves too much, at least unconsciously. But, which mechanisms lie beneath these feelings? If you are shy, you likely have at least one of these two traits:

You Perceive Yourself Negatively

Ask yourself, *why do you feel shy?* You feel like you're embarrassing yourself. You may feel unable to say the right things, ill-prepared for the occasion, unattractive, or simply, downright inadequate. What is yet another common denominator here? Those would be negative self-perceptions. Negative self-perceptions are present when you feel unable to present yourself the way you want to. In your mental structure, there are beliefs about:

- Your actual self, who you think you are

- Your ideal self, who you think you should be, defined by your beliefs about the traits and thoughts that you want to possess

- Your ought self, or whom you believe you are supposed to be. This part of you contains all the traits you believe you should have, but don't.

If you have a negative self-image or low self-esteem, linked to an array of emotional afflictions from anxiety to depression, the different self-structures are in a bit of a conflict. In shyness, your belief of the "actual self" is likely very negative, followed by unrealistic expectations when it comes to the other two self-perceptions.

Believing that you don't possess the abilities that you think you can, cause shyness and anxiety. Either consciously or unconsciously, you don't believe you have the qualities you perceive to be necessary to feel adequate. This feeling results in negative assumptions such as unintelligence, incompetence, or unattractiveness. It becomes reinforced as you're processing selective information feeding into that belief.

You Put All Your Attention on You

When attention is turned inwards during a social event, you will have an excessively negative self-image that you believe to be accurate. In a social situation, people with SAD turn their attention inwards and focus on monitoring and observing themselves. You analyze your sensations and behaviors instead of partaking in social activities. The images and observations you create here are often negative, and you believe them to be accurate. You view yourself from another's perspective, albeit inaccurately. When you practice focusing attention on the environment, the anxiety relieves, and there are fewer negative beliefs. Achieving this however, is easier said than done. In the following sections, you'll learn more about the physiology behind shyness and what you can do to overcome it.

What Happens to Your Mind and Body When You Are Shy?

The physical sensations one has when feeling shy is similar to feeling anxious but less intense. You feel like your cheeks are flushing, you avoid eye contact, and your heart rate increases. Behind this lies psychological elements you wouldn't think have anything to do with your social performance, as they sound like they're coming straight from a CEO's self-improvement guidebook.

Unrealistic Goals and Expectations

Wait. Aren't goals only for people with leather planners or briefcases who want to become millionaires? Not exclusively. Human minds are purpose-oriented, and everything we do, we do with a goal in mind. However, when it comes to social interactions, people without anxiety have a goal to have fun, achieve things, find out information, get out of a speeding ticket, etc. However, with anxiety, your "social goals" mainly revolve around self-image, as it's one of the sore spots and a primary point of focus that takes away the majority of your mental space. One of the reasons for shyness, aside from factors already mentioned, is having unrealistic expectations for yourself in a social situation.

Goals that you set for yourself (e.g., leave a good impression, act smart, come across as intelligent, etc.) determine the standards you set for the situation. For example, when you plan to give a presentation, you set a high standard for yourself to provide ground-breaking information and be eloquent above average. These standards create a set of unrealistic expectations that set off cognitive and physiological responses that correspond to anxiety. Then, these highly-set goals influence your behaviors and cognition. In this case, you are using the information-processing pattern that doesn't help the achievement of goals. Before making a decision, most people choose between a multitude of courses and make plans to achieve goals in certain situations. What does this mean?

Goal setting has multiple phases. In an introduction phase, you are planning and setting your goals. The tricky part about this, particularly with anxiety, is that people tend to set excessively demanding goals to compensate for feeling inadequate. If you're planning a speech, nothing shorter than a Nobel-prize-worthy one, satisfies your criteria. If you're planning to go out, you're not good enough unless you look like a Hollywood star. While people without anxiety don't worry about these things, you, on the other hand, tend to set goals for yourself that are too high, or even impossible to achieve. The problem with this type of goal-setting is that it creates perfectionist expectations. Again, these expectations are too high and unattainable, driven by the perfectionism that is typical for anxiety.

Avoidance

In the execution phase, that is when the trouble happens. Lead by unrealistically set goals, and under the influence of self-defeating elements like self-criticism, negative self-talk, and perfectionism, you freeze. You identify that there's no possibility of meeting the set goals as they're already too high, and so your insecurities get triggered. Perhaps, you wouldn't be insecure about asking your crush out on a date if you didn't set such a high standard for yourself in terms of appearance, social performance, social status, etc. In this case, the reason why you get shy is that you've raised the demands for it to an unachievable level. From there, behaviors like safety behaviors, self-sabotage, and avoidance occur as a result of standards that are too high.

Negative Self-Evaluation

In the evaluation phase, you evaluate your achievement. How well do you think you did? How good did you look? Did you say or do anything wrong? In anxiety and particularly social anxiety, there is a tendency towards exaggerated negative self-evaluation. If you escaped or avoided the situation, you use self-defeating language to label yourself a "loser" or "incompetent," even though none of these are true. If you've pushed through the situation, you tend to feel like you underperformed or embarrassed yourself, even if you didn't.

In the post-action phase, you contemplate your success or failure. With social anxiety, people tend to feel like they failed even if they didn't. If not that, they tend to criticize themselves over the perceived flaws and inadequacies they displayed. For example, if you pass an oral examination successfully or give a presentation, you'll look back at some parts that you considered embarrassing and wallow over them. Although it may have been satisfied the criteria, you may feel like you failed.

Each of these phases has a specific mindset that requires certain types of information to process when rating achievement. In the first stage, the mindset is deliberate and examines the possibilities for progress and desirability of goals. In phase two, you implement a mindset where you process goals preferentially. People without anxiety tend to be optimistic at this stage. Still, those with social anxiety have an exaggerated, negative mindset when it comes to deliberative goal setting and figuring out what to do. Their mindset is most often inappropriate or ill-adjusted to the actions needed to get results. As a result, people with SAD have deficiencies in achieving goals, but also in setting and defining goals and tasks.

Shyness in Children and Adolescents

Shyness is usually present in the process of growing up. But, how can we tell that a child, or an adolescent is too shy? (Hirshfeld-Becker, 2007)

Children

Most children are shy from time to time. It's common for children to shy away from strangers, but become comfortable when they get to know new people. The difference in whether or not the child is shy to a normal or concerning degree is whether or not the child is inhibited. A child who isn't overly shy is outgoing and outspoken most of the time. As you might be familiar, the healthier the child, the likelier the number of mischief and awkward situations where they're blunt and inconsiderate of the appropriateness of their words. However, when shyness becomes a child's behavioral pattern, it's a cause for concern.

An inhibited child won't only cover their eyes or cling onto you for a couple of minutes once you introduce them into a new environment. They are constrained, nervous, and unwilling to socialize way beyond the notion of simply being independent. They actively avoid socializing. I remember thinking that my sister will never make friends if she continues to be withdrawn as she is. She was a constrained child who started showing signs of impairment very early. These signs included:

- Reluctance to interact, which came in the way of developing healthy social skills and friendships

- Withdrawal from group activities and all activities that included performance and being the center of attention, including school

- Highly anxious behavior that can leave you in constant worry of upsetting a child to the point of an emotional breakdown with a single misunderstood sentence

- Constant physical manifestations of feeling ashamed, trembling, stammering, and blushing

However, it is a positive side to shyness that often keeps families from responding in time. As mentioned multiple times throughout this book, my sibling's affliction had positive traits that were much appreciated, like:

- Never getting in trouble

- Being quiet and obedient

- Overall easy to handle

Had my family know just how much hurt is behind those "difficult," mischievous children, I doubt they'd be as accepting of my sister's constraint the way they were. A mentally healthy child exercises all their abilities, including those to stand up for themselves, fight, and talk back. Indeed, those are to be cultivated, as a child must learn to be considerate and respectful of others as well. But, an inhibited child who is shy to the point of concern tends to be very self-critical, and blame everything on themselves, including the words and events that have nothing to do with them.

How to Help an Inhibited Child

If you suspect that your child is shy beyond normal, don't take it as a sign of good childrearing and politeness. I encourage you to support your child by doing the following things:

- **Be kind and patient.** A child who looks constrained and inhibited already judge themselves harshly. Any mishaps they make are nothing but a result of being nervous and tense. Talk to your child in a quiet voice and be understanding of their emotional outbursts. Show interest and approval for them to speak out about how they feel.

- **Encourage socialization.** While most children are hard to keep inside the house, an inhibited child is hard to get out of one. In this case, make gentle, considerate, yet consistent efforts to encourage your child to socialize. Invite other children into your home, and make sure that they spend as much time as possible around other children.

- **Seek professional help.** If it looks like you're not making progress with your child, take them to a school counselor or a therapist. They will help your child learn relaxation and social skills, helping them to repair the damaged self-image, and improve low self-esteem.

Teenagers

Being a teenager is always uncomfortable. Teenagers are otherwise self-aware, and wary about others' opinions of their looks, intelligence, and social skills. However, a teenager who is too shy might start to become withdrawn, which isn't typical behavior for this age group. Shyness is often harder to detect in teens than other age groups because they tend to act shy around adults and authority figures. However, observe whether or not the teenager enjoys or makes efforts to socialize. If the teenager acts inhibited and constrained, avoiding eye contact, and speaking so quietly as for you to barely hear their voice, this could be a cause for concern.

Adolescent shyness that has psychological roots can both result from and cause damaged self-confidence and poor self-esteem. Teenagers are certain to have their share of challenges, but they shouldn't impact the adolescent to the degree to which they'll completely lose interest in socializing.

The one advantage of talking to a teenager over a young child is they understand more complex ideas, so you can share your concern with them in a kind, loving, and supportive way. Here's how to talk to a teenager about shyness:

- Voice your support for them to have an active, fun, outgoing lifestyle

- Tell them you noticed they stopped enjoying going out

- Explain to them why making friends their age is important and how social skills are taught. Let them know that making mistakes is normal

- Ask them about their fears, but be respectful if they don't want to talk about them

- Suggest creating mutual plans for them to socialize more. Acknowledge their choices and preferences, making sure they understand that their wellbeing and comfort are your primary concern

When talking to a teenager about shyness, account for their fear of being the center of attention, being rejected, ridiculed, or judged. If the adolescent voices their concerns, offer your practical help in showing them how to dress, act, and talk. As with the younger age group, don't hesitate to seek expert advice if your teenager doesn't seem to make any improvement.

How to Overcome Shyness?

Exposure Treatment

Exposure is a type of therapy where you confront situations that threaten you. When it comes to shyness, these situations can include shopping, as you might be too self-aware, and feel like people are watching your every move. Upon facing these situations regardless of feeling shy, you master social performance and learn that the experience wasn't nearly as threatening as you thought it would be. The focus of exposure therapy is to experience and see that you, indeed, can go through social situations without adverse outcomes. The more you repeat exposure, the more the anxiety decreases over time.

If you avoid speaking in public because you are afraid your mind will go blank, then examine the two chances of that happening and why you think it will. This will give you an estimate of the possibilities of that happening by looking into what causes your mind to go blank. For example, you can think about briefly losing focus on the topic, which is something that can happen to anyone, not just a person with anxiety. This small mishap can also occur if you haven't been tending to your own needs before the presentation, and you showed up disorganized, tired, sleepy, or hungry. After this, you will be able to make an accurate assessment of the chances of having a mishap, but you'll also be aware that, even if it happens, it's not a disaster. You will realize that there are far more chances of having a successful, pleasant experience instead of a social catastrophe. This exercise is called a technique for challenging catastrophic thinking.

When you practice this technique, your therapist will ask you to define what makes a situation disastrous. Your answer would be something like making a fool out of yourself or embarrassing yourself. However, assuming that something will create a disaster means that you're making assumptions about what other people think. Then, your therapist will ask you to evaluate how do you truly know what other people are thinking about you. They will help you understand that there is no way for you to guess how another person feels about you before they speak their minds. They will also help you understand that your assumptions are inaccurate, meaning that if everyone is out to get you, the world is a hostile place, and that everyone automatically thinks negative of you isn't true. It could be true that certain environments are hostile and toxic, but your assumptions aren't a general rule that applies to all occasions.

Your therapist will help you understand that other people's thinking mainly revolves around them and not you. Even if malicious people surround you, you can work around strategies to manage or minimize your contact with them. Next, they will review with you or simulate what will happen if a hostile or socially challenging situation truly happens. How will you feel? Can the outcomes indeed be so catastrophic, as for you to be unable to survive? They'll guide you through frustrating, embarrassing situations to help you understand that nothing bad can happen, nor did it occur in your previous experiences. You survived, and people didn't think badly of you.

While you are still planning your treatment, your therapist will ask you to create the exercises for exposure and purposefully make social mishaps so that you can examine their actual outcomes. However, the goal is the behavior, and not how you feel during the process.

You will also practice exposure as homework, meaning that you'll do the exercises on your own, in a planned-out, safe way. You will receive a monitoring form about your perceived social costs and risk probability that you associate with these situations. The goal of these exercises is for you to understand that your perceptions of the so-called social cost have been exaggerated and inaccurate.

You are required to evaluate a couple of crucial aspects when you are reviewing your expectations of social threats and mishaps. First, you question what evidence you have that your belief is truthful. Next, based on your previous experience, you evaluate how often or whether or not the situation had ever happened. You will ask yourself what the worst things that can occur are, and in case they do, will you be able to cope with them? While the first two questions identify your errors in thinking, the second helps you determine your catastrophic thinking and create a more balanced impression of the situations.

Repeated exposure during treatment helps you improve emotional control. Exposure is similar to the acceptance technique. It enables you to go through the experience of anxiety and understand that you can survive it instead of resorting to avoidant behaviors. It means to be open to the experiences of the present moment regardless of pleasantness. There's plenty of scientific evidence to confirm that those with SAD think they have weaker social skills than they do. The perception of your social skills determines your confidence in a situation. You most likely perceive yourself to be inadequate, assuming that you'll act inadequately in a situation, regardless of whether or not this is accurate. These are a wide range of behaviors that people use to avoid focusing on anxiety, as they believe that they can reduce it. Safety and avoidant behaviors are only feeding to the fear of social situations and can be eliminated with exposure. To identify them, you need to monitor your own social experiences. You benefit from treating avoidant behaviors because the more you engage in social situations without using these behaviors, the more your anxiety symptoms will reduce.

To do this, you will first create a hierarchy list of fear and avoidance. You will first list the ten most provoking situations, and the behavior you are using to calm yourself down. Next, you should evaluate to which degree you can avoid a situation. You can also look into factors that contribute to the anxiety, like the number of people, the setting, or the performance.

Cognitive Behavioral Therapy (CBT)

In CBT, you examine the way you think about social situations. With a therapist, you review your thinking pattern before, during, and after a social situation that triggers anxiety. With CBT, you question a couple of important aspects of your mindset, such as:

- What are adequate and inadequate behaviors, and how suitable are your actions to a situation?

- Is it true or rational that people perceive you as negatively as you think?

- What core belief causes you to think negatively about yourself, and is it accurate and rational?

This way, you change your mindset about yourself and your social performance. Similarly to exposure therapy, after you've reviewed your mindset with a therapist, you then proceed with actions to challenge fears and negative beliefs. Challenging beliefs helps you build new coping skills on the successful experiences you had.

Learn How to Relax

Applied relaxation teaches you how to relax when you feel shy. With this treatment, you learn correct breathing and self-affirming techniques to help you calm down instantly, stopping the flow of fear, insecurity, and self-defeating thoughts at the moment.

If you're suffering from social anxiety, you likely exaggerate the negativity and perceived risks from a social situation. One of the reasons you have anxiety is that you think that there are reasons for you to be anxious or afraid. One of the goals in cognitive therapy is for you to think more realistically. If the situation is bad, refusing to feel so means that you are refusing to be aware of the reality. However, if the severity of the situation isn't as grave as you think it is, that means that your anxiety is an exaggerated reaction, often caused by automatic, intrusive thoughts.

A lot of people have trouble identifying automatic and maladaptive thoughts because they appear accurate to them. This is why conversation is important for you to review and question your reasoning for making certain evaluations. Maladaptive thoughts classify into dysfunctional beliefs and negative automatic thoughts. Dysfunctional beliefs are assumptions you create about people, the world, and yourself on criteria that are mainly irrational and inaccurate.

For example, you may believe that you have to be pleasant company and you have to sound eloquent or say something funny to be accepted. Not only is that false, but you won't always be in the mood to act this way if they aren't your natural traits. Perhaps you enjoy listening more than talking, and you never have to keep up the laughs as much as you think. You also think that not having the perceived desired traits means that you are worthless.

These assumptions are based on the irrational belief that you will be remodeling during the cognitive-behavioral treatment. You'll aim to set up realistic standards when it comes to measuring what is necessary and acceptable in a social situation.

People with other anxiety-related disorders tend to lack a sense of reasonable standard in social performance and situations. They are perfectionists in all areas of their life. The irrational beliefs are making you feel very inadequate and very anxious in social situations. As a result, you might be avoiding social contact. Avoidance can cause you to form unrealistic goals and expectations from yourself. In social anxiety, there is a typical set of irrational beliefs. These cause you to exaggerate the probability of underestimating the chances of an embarrassing outcome. While doing CBT exercises, you will be asked to evaluate whether or not the perceived risk is truly realistic. For example, if you feel that your mind will go blank while giving a presentation, and you'll embarrass yourself, you are to evaluate whether or not that had ever really happened. The chances are that it never happened or if it did, it only happened for a second, after which you managed to regain your focus and proceed with your speech.

Chapter 5: How to Stop Panic Attacks

Often, the symptoms of panic attacks can feel like a heart attack, leaving the person afraid for their life. Many people who experience panic attacks go to the emergency room, as they believe that their life is threatened. If the condition goes without therapy, occasional panic attacks can grow into a panic disorder. A panic disorder is characterized by continuous panic attacks that result in significant changes in behaviors, quality of life impairment, and the increase of overall anxiety. While a panic disorder isn't the same as social anxiety, some similarities between the two can leave you confused. Here's how to know if you have a panic disorder:

- You have frequent, regular panic attacks

- You're avoiding activities you used to enjoy because of fear of panic attacks, and you start to behave significantly different.

Panic attempts can cause a lot of emotional distress, leaving you feeling down and damaging your self-esteem. This can cause the development of the so-called anticipatory anxiety when you're in constant fear and anticipation of panic attacks. This can disable you and limit you significantly. Panic attacks can also lead to phobic avoidance, which is a state in which you start avoiding particular environments and situations that you think might cause the attacks.

Treatment

You may feel like you can't control your panic attacks, but it is achievable with practice and persistence. There are a couple of techniques that you can use to treat panic attacks:

Avoid Stimulants

Make sure to quit alcohol, caffeine, and smoking. If you're sensitive to panic attacks, these substances can increase the risks. Also, pay attention to reduce any other beverages, such as energy drinks and other medications that stimulate your nervous system.

Practice Breathing

Having control over your breath will help you calm down and reduce the symptoms of overwhelming fear and panic. Many of the other symptoms, such as dizziness, shaking, and feeling out of breath, happen due to hyperventilation. When your breathing is deep and even, these sensations will also subside. Practicing proper breathing will help you relieve anxiety and feel more in control over your body.

Learn How to Relax

Regular relaxation will help your body exercise calming responses that oppose the reactions to the stress experienced in a panic attack. These exercises include meditation, yoga, and muscle relaxation. Aside from helping you relax, these exercises also help you feel more joyful and in harmony.

Practice Connection

Anxiety, including its social form, often comes with detachment from your inner being and the outside world. In this sense, your ability to connect, whether with people, your feelings, or physical sensations is compromised. Fearing panic attacks often leads to isolation, which only increases the disorder, whether you're talking about anxiety, social anxiety, or panic. Building supportive relationships will help you feel like you're being loved and cared for. Remember, social anxiety boils down to how you were treated as a child. The response you received to vocalizing your needs resulted in forming different types of childhood attachment. Overall, there are four types of attachment a child can form with their main caregivers that later reflect on their relationships with themselves and other people.

Safe attachment, which is considered necessary for a healthy state of mind, is nurtured by unconditional love, responsiveness, and support from the main caregivers.

Usually, people who have anxiety fall in one of the three remaining categories that represent insecure attachment: Avoidant, anxious, and disorganized attachment share a different degree of disconnecting oneself from their own sensations, suppressing. This happens when, for different reasons, you start to withdraw from asking love, support, and company when you need it.

SAD links to insecure attachment styles because you form an ambivalent relationship with people: On the one hand, you want to be close to friends, family, and coworkers, because you need love, friendship, and company. You shy away from making these connections because you feel unworthy of acceptance. Feeling unworthy of acceptance goes back to early infancy, when crying for consolation or shouting out of confusion and insecurity brought you shame and criticism. However, as a conscious person, you can practice making connections to overcome emotional blockages due to feeling unworthy. You can do this in following ways:

- **Socialize, even when you don't feel like it.** The only way for the anxiety to go away is to persist socializing despite feeling awkward.

- **Practice seeking emotional support.** Overly self-critical people tend to deny themselves help and support when they need it the most, further worsening the feeling of detachment from the outside world. Commit to contacting at least one person when you feel upset. Choose a friend or a family member who can understand your condition and is capable of giving rational feedback, but still cares about you and can offer understanding and consolation.

- **Don't refuse help.** Chances are that you rarely, if ever, ask for help at work or at home, and delay seeking medical help until your symptoms become critical. Refusing help is typical for all forms of anxiety and depression. The desire to do everything by yourself arises from feeling incompetent and from having an exaggerated perception of standards for competence and success. Learning how to ask for and accept help will help you normalize your social standards, and bring you closer with people around you.

Physical Exercise

Regular exercise for 30 minutes a day can significantly reduce panic and anxiety symptoms. You can choose among the many practices you like, such as aerobic exercise, walking, or rhythmic exercises.

Good Sleep

Poor sleep is proven to increase the symptoms of anxiety and depression. With social anxiety, it's common to lose sleep over post-event rumination and fears related to carrying out the plans for the following day. Both anxiety and depression link to insomnia. Being sleep-deprived increases your stress-hormone levels, further intensifying the symptoms of anxiety, such as an increased heart rate, confusion, and the inability to focus. By getting more quality sleep, you'll relax more, and your body will release less stress hormones, and more brain chemicals responsible for feeling satisfied, like serotonin. However, getting good quality sleep is more challenging than it may seem. When you're constantly upset, it's hard to fall asleep and stay asleep. For these reasons, people with anxiety usually stay up late, only to sleep in the following day. This pattern sets you up for an unproductive day, which only increases your insecurity. To overcome social anxiety, you'll also need to establish good sleeping habits.

The better you sleep, the more relaxed and productive you'll feel. But, how can you do this with so many unpleasant thoughts rushing through your head? Here are a couple of tips to change your sleep habits and secure more quality sleep:

- Pay attention to get between seven and nine hours of sleep each day.

- Unwind early. Set aside at least two hours without screen time or housework before going to bed. This will help quiet your mind and fall asleep faster.

- Reduce caffeine and alcohol. Caffeinated and alcoholic drinks disturb healthy sleep, even if you don't have insomnia. Avoid these brain stimulants at least a couple of hours before going to bed.

- Release negative thoughts and energy. You can plan out a relaxing evening routine that includes a light dinner, a bath, some reading, and a cup of your favorite healthy drink, like a glass of milk, cocoa, or tea. If you enjoy mindfulness, you can also journal or meditate.

What Are the Most Effective Treatments for Panic Disorder?

Cognitive Behavioral Therapy (CBT)

CBT treatment helps you change the way you think and discover the actual thoughts that are triggering your panic attacks. More importantly, CBT enables you to track the thinking patterns that lead to panic attacks. When practicing CBT for panic attacks, you will monitor the situation to discover the actual thoughts that caused the physical sensations.

Exposure

Exposure helps you experience a panic attack in a safe environment, where there's no possibility of anything harmful happening to you. This way, you learn how to cope with the symptoms. During exposure, you may be asked to purposefully hyperventilate, hold your breath, or voluntarily shake, to show that no harm will come out of it. By simulating a panic attack, your fear of the symptoms reduces. You're no longer as afraid of the sensations, and you start to feel like you can control the panic. Depending on the type of disorder you have, exposure can refer to specific situations that trigger the attacks. You may practice entering the situation where the panic attacks usually occur. By going through these situations, you learn that you can cope, and you build confidence.

Medication

Medication can be useful to ease your symptoms temporarily. However, they're not a long-term solution for the disorder. For the medication to be effective you also need to make lifestyle changes and practice other forms of therapy that address the true causes. You may get prescribed antidepressants or benzodiazepines. As benzodiazepines are highly addictive, you'll most likely get a prescription only if extremely necessary.

How to Practice CBT for Panic Attacks

CBT is a technique that was proven best in helping prevent and overcoming panic attacks. It is a goal-oriented technique that examines your thinking and behavioral patterns. CBT examines how your thoughts trigger feelings and are influenced by your perceptions. Based on these insights, you can see how your thoughts affect your behavior and what you can do to alter your perceptions about a situation and bring them to a more positive and balanced level. While you may not always be able to adjust your lifestyle to feel better, as many people can't change their work, surroundings, or health, you can change the way you think and respond to these situations, so you feel calmer and more in control.

CBT revolves around changing the flaws in your thinking that led to anxiety, depression, and panic attacks. Technically, CBT observes that your panic attack is triggered by your thoughts, observations, and evaluations of a situation. This way, CBT helps you overcome negative thinking patterns that are harming your health and causing panic attacks.

What Makes You Vulnerable to Panic Attacks?

According to CBT, you are prone to panic attacks because you're influenced by negative, self-defeating thoughts and beliefs that result from damaged self-esteem and a negative self-image. You'll work on the root causes of panic attacks in the long run, but to start, you'll work towards building the skills to cope with panic attacks and enforcing your sense of emotional and mental control. Here's how CBT for panic attacks works:

Identifying Negative Thoughts

In CBT, emotional, physical, and behavioral responses are considered to arise from thoughts. These thoughts can flow swiftly through your mind, and you're unable to catch them, so you feel like the attack came out-of-the-blue. To determine this, your therapist will ask you to recall everything about the situation, from the setting, to how you felt and what you were thinking at the time. There are numerous ways to become aware of negative thoughts and replace them with positive ones. Your therapist might recommend the thought record, the evidence technique, or journaling. They will also give you homework so you can track your thinking and get insight into your thought process.

One of the easiest ways to discover your negative thinking patterns is with writing exercises, like keeping a panic diary, journaling, affirmations, and gratitude journaling. These techniques enable you to be more aware of the positives in your life while acknowledging the negatives.

Improving Coping Skills and Behaviors

Healthy coping skills enable you to find better ways to cope with overwhelming feelings so that they don't cause a panic attack. Your therapist will show you the techniques for relaxation, managing anxiety, and dealing with panic attacks.

However, the most important part of CBT for panic disorder is the exposure or the so-called desensitization. By engaging in the events you find triggering, and going through them with the therapist's guidelines for proper coping, you teach your body and mind not to respond with anxiety. As your brain learns that the situation isn't truly threatening, it stops creating the physiological responses that cause panic. Systematic desensitization gradually introduces you to anxiety-inducing situations while showing you how to manage. You start from the least "threatening" situations, moving up to the most. With this exercise, you're required to use relaxation techniques that the therapist demonstrates, that will help you relieve tension, calm down, lower your heart rate, relieve fears, and improve skills to cope with problems. These techniques include yoga, progressive muscle relaxation, and breathing exercises.

Panic Attacks in Children and Adolescents

Both children and adolescents can succumb to panic attacks. Their symptoms are similar to those of adults. While panic disorder can develop in childhood, it mainly starts in adolescence. The panic disorder can run in families, and it can have a devastating impact on the lives of children. When it comes to adolescents, panic attacks can get in the way of school, relationships, and healthy psychological development.

Children with panic attacks can become insecure, reluctant to go out and socialize, and ashamed of having panic attacks. They can even become afraid of leaving their house.

For example, if school triggers distressing thoughts for a child, they may start to avoid going to school or keep to themselves while in class. This can get in the way of academic success. Children with untreated panic disorder can also develop agoraphobia, which is a fear of open spaces. Teens and adolescents, however, can resort to substance abuse to ease the impact of the disorder and cope with panic attacks.

Because children and adolescents are very ashamed and secretive about their panic attacks, diagnosing them with the disorder can be difficult.

In addition, children are unable to identify that their experiences are mental, so they might be frequently admitted to the emergency room or treated for physical conditions. Luckily, panic attacks in children and adolescents are equally treatable as adults'. Children and teens can undergo psychotherapy, cognitive behavioral therapy, receive appropriate medication, and use self-help techniques to overcome the panic attacks.

Panic Attacks in Women

Women tend to experience panic attacks 2.5 times more than men. This means that women are part of the population that is most susceptible to the panic disorder. Panic attacks are most frequent in women ages between 15 and 24 but remain higher than those in men across all age groups. In addition, women tend to report a more intense sensation of the most distressing physical sensations in panic attacks, like feeling smothered, shortness of breath, and an increased heart rate.

While researchers haven't yet confirmed the exact explanation of why women are more prone to panic attacks, there are a couple of possible explanations. It's assumed that the fluctuations of estrogen and progesterone throughout a woman's menstrual cycle can increase the symptoms of panic attacks during the premenstrual stage. It was also found that the women who had premenstrual dysphoria, a severe form of premenstrual syndrome, experienced more frequent and severe panic attacks. A direct connection was found between the fluctuation of estrogen and hyperventilation, which tends to affect women a lot more than men when it comes to panic attacks.

In this chapter, you learned more about panic attacks. Unlike anxiety attacks that create a fear of embarrassment and the desire to run away, panic attacks have a greater physical impact. When experiencing a panic attack, you might start to feel like your health in danger. You might feel like you can't breathe like you're about to faint or have a heart attack. Luckily, panic attacks are temporary and should subside anywhere from 10 to 30 minutes. The reasons for panic attacks are psychological. Your thoughts, beliefs, and assumptions related to the situation can cause a surge of overwhelming feelings that may appear too intense to cope with. Alongside a therapist, you can work to shed light on these feelings. More than that, you can use exposure, relaxation techniques, and CBT, to discover the root causes of your panic attacks and learn how to cope with them. Panic attacks could affect both men and women, as well as children, teenagers, and adults.

However, women are more vulnerable to panic attacks because of hormonal fluctuations throughout the menstrual cycle. The most important thing to remember is that panic attacks aren't caused directly by the triggering situation. They are caused by the thoughts and feelings you associate with a situation, and beliefs and assumptions you carry about yourself.

Workbook: Panic Attack CBT Worksheets

Keeping track of your panic attacks will help you identify triggers and assume more control over emotional and physical reactions. One of the reasons why panic attacks are so frightening is because they are seemingly unpredictable, and make you feel powerless to cope with physical sensations. These worksheets are useful for learning the patterns of triggering situations.

When do you experience panic attacks? Panic attacks usually happen in similar conditions and situations. Knowing which situations typically trigger a panic attack will help you prepare mentally and physically, which will increase your confidence and reduce avoidance of social situations.

How intense is your fear? You'll be able to observe sensations and emotional reactions, identifying those that affect you the most. Rating and scaling situations that trigger panic attacks will help you create strategies to face and manage these situations, like using breathing techniques, taking a break, finding someone to talk to, etc.

What are you thinking about? Usually, thoughts surrounding panic attacks revolve around fear for one's life due to different irrational ideas. According to CBT, thoughts you're unwilling to acknowledge, either because they're too frightening or hurtful, trigger panic attacks. By tracking these thoughts, associating them with situations, and comparing the physical sensations they cause, you'll begin to understand what the self-destructive thought patterns you want to overcome are.

What are your coping strategies? By tracking the behaviors you usually use to cope with panic attacks, you'll be able to distinguish those that are helpful from those that are not. This way, you can exercise doing more of the things that help you calm down, like reassuring yourself that you are doing well, and use fewer avoidant behaviors, such as making excuses to leave, or drinking alcohol to calm down.

You can use this CBT worksheet to reflect and learn from panic attacks, plan strategies to manage symptoms, or as a part of CBT treatment. By looking into your worksheet, your therapist will design exposure exercises, which revolve around facing and overcoming fears. It will also help them examine your thought patterns and discover negative core beliefs that are causing anxiety and panic attacks.

Date & Time				
Situation (Describe in detail)				
Fear (Rate from 0 to 100)				
Thoughts (Before, during, and after)				
Coping Strategies (What did you do to manage this situation?)				

Chapter 6: How to Build Your Self-Esteem and Self Confidence

I've witnessed how low self-esteem can both cause and fuel anxiety. While I didn't yet fully understand the relationship between social anxiety and SAD, I knew that my dear sister didn't have the confidence to appreciate herself for who she was. She was and still is smart, talented, and profoundly likable. However, the more she stemmed away from society, the worse she felt about herself. I could see her efforts to break out of her shell, but her choices and actions said otherwise. I could tell that my sister had high expectations of herself, but very little faith in her abilities. Before my research, I was only able to understand that she's too hard on herself. Talking to her sometimes felt like listening to two people arguing. She'd defend herself from made-up judgment and attacks, ruminate and talk about irrelevant gossip and rumors on her account, and always felt threatened. Where did this come from, I wondered?

A lesson that I soon learned was that social anxiety has a huge connection with self-esteem. It not only puts you at greater risk of social anxiety but also increases the effects of the disorder. Simply experiencing social anxiety can make you feel a lot worse about yourself. The more you struggle with social anxiety, the more your self-esteem suffers. A significant part of overcoming social fear requires looking into your self-worth. Combined with social anxiety, low self-esteem can further reinforce your negative self-image self-esteem and core beliefs. Those with SAD have negative core beliefs about themselves and the disorder. For example, you might believe that you can't control your anxiety around other people, or that you don't have the right skills to perform while in reality, these beliefs are rooted in low self-esteem and can reinforce the disorder.

Everyone makes mistakes. However, the majority of people are able to recover and bounce back. If you have low self-esteem, it may seem like the way you feel in a particular situation determines the way you think of yourself in general. The way you feel about yourself and what you believe about yourself depends on the situation. So it's very easy for you to spiral into negativity. Those who have healthy self-esteem can evaluate themselves accurately and estimate their strengths, weaknesses, and they also believe they are worthy people, regardless of those.

Self-esteem is a personality trait that reflects your sense of self-worth. If you have high levels of self-esteem, you have a healthy sense of your worth. You understand that you deserve good things in life, such as happiness, love, satisfaction, and success. You don't expect or feel entitled to the good things in life, but you profoundly believe that you are worthy of them. People with healthy self-esteem are usually the happiest and most successful, as they tend to measure and evaluate their performance and actions accurately. However, this sense of self-worth isn't grandiose. You don't believe that you're better than other people in any way; you think that you are good enough, capable of doing both right and wrong.

People with a grandiose self or sense of self-worth are often called narcissists, while those with a deficient feeling of self-worth tend to suffer from depression and anxiety. If you have SAD that means your self worth is most likely compromised. You should be working towards improving self-esteem and self-confidence. As you can see, neither extremely high nor extremely low sense of confidence is healthy. You should work towards developing a healthy sense of self-worth that is a balanced measure of understanding your good traits and personal strengths, as well as limitations and challenges.

The Root of Low Self-Esteem

If you know you have low self-esteem, look into the cause. Perhaps, you can recall a specific time in life when you started feeling bad about yourself. Adverse experiences that cause low self-esteem usually happen in childhood, and they include parental criticism, physical or sexual abuse, and emotional neglect. Being teased or bullied, ridiculed, or having other people having unrealistic standards and unrealistically high expectations of you might also be the root of any issues.

Those who have healthy self-esteem usually grow up feeling validated, loved, heard, accepted, and respected. This category of people usually develops a healthy self-image. However, if your upbringing was challenging, even if you had loving parents and positive experiences, you could grow up with self-esteem problems.

Inner Criticism

Everyone has an inner voice that serves to evaluate them. One of the ways to test your self-esteem is to look at what your inner voice is saying. If this voice shares thoughts of reassurance and acceptance, it is most likely that you have a healthy self-esteem. However, if it's the opposite, if that inner voice is criticizing or belittling you, you may have self-esteem issues.

Research proved that people with social anxiety associate negative words with themselves more than positive words. This means that if you have social anxiety, you are less likely to believe in the positives about yourself. Science also proved that people with social anxiety usually have lower self-esteem than those without it. Another study showed that low self-esteem could result in behaviors known as self-verification, where people tend to seek and prefer negative feedback unconsciously. (Antony, 2000)

When an inner voice is telling you negative things about yourself, you'll put yourself in situations that are a self-fulfilling prophecy. The more you think negatively about yourself, the more you unconsciously seek situations that will confirm that image. Instead of looking for ways to encourage yourself and boost self-esteem, you are looking for ways to verify negative self-image, instead of stopping to feed into that critical voice, you are looking to validate it. This allows self-criticism to grow stronger.

How the Cycle of Low Self-Esteem Works

Aside from having a high perception of social standards, you also have trouble choosing and maintaining attainable goals. This is because you set goals based on achievable criteria. One of those beliefs could be that you must always perform perfectly, or you must be put together, and always look your best to be accepted. These unrealistic expectations create pressure, and you resort to avoidance. Because your expectations are impractical, and any lower expectations don't satisfy the perceived societal standards, you will resort to safety behaviors.

When this cycle ends, another begins. The more you repeat this behavioral pattern, the more you feed into social anxiety and further worsen your self-esteem. For example, choosing to stay at home instead of going to a party or going to work can make you feel temporarily better, but in the long run, it makes you feel worse about yourself and your abilities, you start to feel like you are unworthy or incompetent or lazy for doing that. As a result, your self-esteem suffers, and your social anxiety increases.

How Does SAD Interact With Low Self-Esteem?

As you have learned by now, people with SAD have unrealistic standards for social functioning and social skills. Once they face a challenging situation, people with SAD tend to shift focus to their symptoms of anxiety and evaluate themselves negatively in terms of social settings. This means that you have a habit of overestimating the negative consequences of a social encounter. With SAD, it is typical for people to believe they don't have control over their emotional responses, and view themselves as socially inadequate, without the skills to cope with situations. As a result, they use dysfunctional strategies, like post-event rumination, safety behaviors, and avoidance. This increases the negative expectations of future events.

What prevents people from breaking their dysfunctional beliefs is that they tend to focus too much on themselves when they enter a social situation. This shift creates an awareness of their anxiety and gets in the way of processing the situation. It produces information that creates negative self-impression, further damaging your self-esteem. Secondly, those with SAD tend to use many safety behaviors to avoid anxiety. This tendency keeps them from critically evaluating the realistic outcomes of dreaded situations and corrects their catastrophic beliefs.

They also exaggerate how negatively they will be viewed and how negatively the situation will unfold. They make more negative predictions of their performance. The disorder-specific CBT model for SAD includes the perceptions of inadequacy due to being overly self-critical and believing in high social standards, goals, and expectations. If there's a need to make particular impressions, people with SAD don't believe they will be able to do it because they are unable to set realistic goals and behavior strategies. This increases self-focused attention and social avoidance. This creates an exaggerated perception of negative results and the severity of possible consequences, consistent with the belief that they will act badly or otherwise inadequately which can induce negative outcomes and responses.

Typically, if you have low self-esteem, you tend to anticipate negative events, such as mishaps and accidents, and you turn to avoidant and safety behaviors to prevent them. After this, you ruminate on the event, further beating yourself up, and the cycle keeps going.

Self-Fulfilling Prophecy

Compromised self-esteem drives you to exaggerate social standards when it comes to making a positive impression. Combined with the belief that your skills aren't good enough to manage, you start to underestimate your abilities, believing that you don't have the personal traits that other successful people have.

When you believe that your standards are accurate, you might even, albeit unconsciously, cause yourself to fail purposefully, so that expectations from you would be lower. Underperforming at work, or avoiding to break free out of your comfort zone and demonstrate your skills at school, are only some of the harmful consequences. In combination with SAD, low self-esteem also causes you to evaluate your performance as being worse than it actually is.

How to Improve Self-Esteem With SAD

Cognitive-Behavioral Therapy

CBT treatments that include exposure, cognitive restructuring and the training of social skills serve to modify safety behaviors and self-focused attention using a wide range of CBT strategies. Cognitive-behavioral treatment is a great way for you to improve self-esteem by changing your mindset and practicing real-life situations that help you understand and appreciate your value.

Cognitive Restructuring

With CBT, you can learn healthy techniques for cognitive restructuring. In this case, you practice identifying negative automatic thoughts by observing the relationship between your emotional responses and thought process.

You can then evaluate your logic and rationality of your beliefs and assumptions, noting the errors in your judgment, and move to formulate more rational alternatives.

Exposure Exercises for Self-Esteem

After reframing your mindset, you can proceed to make real-life experiences that prove the newly-formed, balanced beliefs. This is called a behavior exposure experiment. In these exercises, you confront difficult situations while applying the cognitive restructuring techniques that you learned. After the exercise, it is important to reflect on the situation and make conclusions that deepen the sense of self-value.

Just because you currently have low self-esteem doesn't mean that it has to stay like that for life. There are many things that you can do to improve your self-esteem. You can start by making small changes that will improve how you see yourself. CBT can help both manage the symptoms of SAD and boost your self-esteem, but there are also other things that you can do. However, there is no way that you can go back into the past and correct perceived past wrongdoings with social anxiety.

It is important not to blame yourself for having the disorder, and for having your insecurities hold you back. You should practice accepting that you won't always do things perfectly, and you won't always know the answer; how to navigate feelings or act in every situation. Learn to accept bad feelings. Instead of trying to suppress them or avoid them, forgive yourself for not being perfect and learn how to accept yourself in the present moment. This way, you will gradually increase your self-esteem. Aside from that, you can always practice counseling and therapy and build your self-esteem through the exercise of challenging core beliefs and exposure. Ultimately, exposure and going through the challenging experiences is what builds you up. It helps you learn that you can go beyond your limits and say, do, and experience things you never thought you would.

In this chapter, you learned more about the role of self-esteem in SAD. Low self-esteem plays an essential role in social anxiety, right after the negative core beliefs that shaped your mindset. Having low self-esteem affected your life in numerous negative ways. First, you continuously, yet unconsciously, worked to confirmed negative self-beliefs. A hard idea to grasp is how we're able to subtly navigate our lives in a poor direction to confirm the negative self-image created by low self-esteem. You learned that you did this through perfectionism and unrealistically high expectations you subconsciously knew to be unachievable. The possibility of setting yourself up for failure by using avoidance and self-sabotage, both being unconscious mechanisms. These keep you stuck in place as well as confirm that you're a person unworthy of love, respect, or acceptance.

Combined with perfectionism and unrealistic expectations, avoidance, safety behaviors, and self-sabotage deepen a sense of failure and minimize achieved successes. When an expectation is set too high, there's no possibility of fulfilling it. Whether you avoid or underperform, you are doomed to fail. Failing purposefully, although an unconscious mechanism, is easily achieved through self-sabotage and procrastination. For example, it is possible to purposefully make a simple task so complicated that it is unachievable. This thought pattern causes you to choose tasks and goals beyond your grasp, expecting yourself to succeed but setting yourself up to fail. This can apply to all areas of your life. From applying to jobs that aren't a fit for your skills, to self-sabotage by either procrastinating, or using avoidance mechanisms; From choosing to isolate yourself and not love at all, choosing to love those who are emotionally unavailable, and either mistreat you or don't love you back; From choosing to isolate yourself from friends, comparing yourself with those who are above your perceived social rank, success scale, or "league." All of these behaviors have one common denominator: low self-esteem.

A lack of appreciation for yourself can be deeply hidden behind high aspirations and a truly low perception of your abilities. In this chapter, you learned that there is a way for you to improve self-esteem. It is a simple practice of learning to accept and appreciate yourself but a hard mission for someone fearing ridicule and scrutiny. In order to repair damaged self-esteem, you first need to identify how it shapes your thinking and actions. After that, you need to identify the exact situations that put your self-esteem on a test, triggering extreme anxiety. Upon this, you'll finally be able to build yourself up through real challenges and exposures.

These self-induced experiments help you see that you're a lot more than you think you are, and that you're able to do a lot more than you thought you could. With these experiences, you'll finally be able to leave the negative self-image behind, and start appreciating yourself for what you are - a unique, worthy, valuable person. As you approach the final chapters of this book, you'll learn more about creating a cohesive, step-by-step plan to overcome social anxiety once and for all. In the next chapter, you'll learn how to practice exposure therapy as a way of overcoming SAD.

Chapter 7: How to Overcome Social Anxiety and Change Your Life

In the previous chapter, you learned that low self-esteem is one of the most significant contributing factors to social anxiety. To overcome low self-esteem, it is important to evaluate your logic and rationale. This way, the mistakes you make in your thinking that are driving you to make exaggerated, negative, assumptions, and conclusions. This process is called cognitive restructuring and can be used as an individual treatment, as a part of a wholesome CBT treatment plan, and as an additional treatment to exposure. Exposure is, as you learned, the ultimate way to improve your self-esteem and overcome anxiety (Antony, 2000).

Exposure is in theory, a simple concept. It requires you to face a situation that you fear and learn positive lessons from experience. This is easier said than done, as you're about to learn. It is a lesson that I learned through my efforts to support my recovering sibling. What I learned during my studies was that exposure needs to be carefully designed to be effective. If not, it can be counterproductive. As it turned out, exposure requires meticulous planning, constant self-reflection, and open-mindedness to question your beliefs. This is yet another demanding task since most of us are inclined to hold on to what we believe. We believe what we perceive to be accurate and right, and challenging that leaves us feeling confused, and often lost.

Here's a simple depiction:

If you believe that your abilities are low, you have an idea about what your life and activities should look like to live and survive with that truth. But what if you're wrong? What if you're talented and smart? What if you're even above that? Considering this idea means stepping into a headspace where you no longer understand who you are. Because your life and self-perception are made on the grounds of core beliefs, shaking those can also cause turbulence in the way you see yourself and your life. In this chapter, we'll review the process of performing and applying exposures so that they indeed teach you lessons of self-worth.

How to Plan Exposure

Exposure is also a treatment in which you purposely create a situation that tests your fears. This can be an effective way to test and overcome negative evaluations and assumptions. However, to ensure the beneficial effect of the exposure exercises, one must first create a plan. Planning exposure is necessary to identify the problem, set goals, and define evaluation standards. With that in mind, the three main parts of planning exposure treatment include (Hope, 2004):

Identify the Problem

First, you'll need to examine your thought process to identify what situations trigger anxiety, which thoughts preceded it, and what core beliefs are driving your logic. The mindset needs to be scrutinized to determine and successfully challenge fears and review the perceived risks from social events. People with SAD tend to have a perception of low emotional control, meaning that they feel powerless to manage their emotions. One of the ways to correct this is by creating a distance between the perception of your emotional state and the objective view on yourself from an observer's point of view. This helps you understand that others can't see that you are shivering and that your hands are sweating, relieving the fear that everyone notices your symptoms.

Prevent Safety Behaviors

Next, alongside your therapist, you'll review inadequate coping mechanisms that you use to cope with social anxiety. Safety behaviors are successfully treated during exposures and usually eliminated after a certain number of repetitions. You will detect and review the actions you take to relieve your anxiety, identifying those that shouldn't be used in exposures. Next, you'll work on planning to prevent or reduce, post-event rumination. Post-event rumination treatment is done by learning how to process events using rational reasoning, such as whether your recollection of the event is factually accurate, what is the evidence of the (in)accuracy, and whether or not potential mishaps have any true impact on you and your life.

Design Exposures

To design exposures, you will plan out actions, like going to places and planning events that challenge your false beliefs. This means that the situations need to be specifically designed to target core beliefs, such as:

- That you don't know how to act in a situation

- That other people will be overly critical and negative towards you

- That a social situation will have a catastrophic outcome due to your inadequacy

- These exercises are also great for you to learn that you can cope with the symptoms of anxiety and that the other people aren't noticing them as much as you think they are

For example, you might notice that you don't have to present yourself as perfectly as you thought to be accepted in a group. Another form of exercise includes engaging in a situation while making sure that no safety behaviors are being used. These behaviors make you think that you are somehow relieving the symptoms and protecting yourself from the negative outcome, but this isn't true. These behaviors are preventing you from facing the situation in the way in which you should. This way, you not only survive a situation but also feel good about yourself. These situations may include anything from spilling a drink on purpose or revealing information about yourself that you used to believe people will judge you on.

Relaxation Training

A significant portion of exposure therapy is to learn how to manage physical symptoms of social anxiety. Relaxation training helps you not only relax and feel better but also learn to control mental oversensitivity. Mental oversensitivity becomes high in social situations, and learning how to relax will help you go through the situation a lot easier. Multiple exercises can be used in relaxation training. Some of them target relaxing specific muscles, creating an exposure ladder, and doing the so-called homework, which requires you to write down thoughts and observations on the exercise you perform without a therapist.

With muscle relaxation, you are encouraged to focus on specific muscle groups within your body, noticing the difference in how they feel when they are tight and relaxed. This form of body scanning helps you notice the muscle tension and record how it feels to be relaxed. Relaxation training can also be used in the form of cue-controlled relaxation, which means that you use the word "relax" over and over while you are in a relaxed state. Then you move on to use this approach in your everyday activities.

For example, once you notice that you feel anxious, you then take a couple of deep breaths and repeat yourself to relax. As a result, you learn how to manage your symptoms better and get a hold of yourself when you start to feel like your symptoms are getting out of control.

This technique seems simple, but it needs to be exercised frequently to be effective. It will help you learn how to manage the physical sensations when you are distressed, and eventually, learn how to relax very quickly during everyday activities. After that, you may apply this exercise to the situations that provoke anxiety. As a result, you learn to manage feelings in anxiety-provoking situations.

Learning to Change Anxiety-Provoking Thoughts and Expectations

Social anxiety leads to damage in overall functioning and particularly in terms of social skills, relationships, and career. Dysfunctional core beliefs fuel negative self-evaluation, which is found to enhance anxiety responses. Self- evaluation is one of the strategies of emotional regulation that consists of reframing the context of emotional stimulus so that their impact is changed. Technically, you can work towards changing the meaning of sensations to alter the effect of the emotion. Those with SAD have been proven to share lower blood oxygen level-dependent signaling response to attention and cognitive control. They also show delayed activation of the prefrontal cortex and lesser functional connectivity of the amygdala. Simply put, this means that those with a SAD take a bit longer to evaluate their own experiences properly. Before responding, you need to step back and think through your reaction to a situation, analyzing it from a rational point of view. For example, when you feel anxious about asking for medicine out loud at a pharmacy, you can step back and analyze your sensations. You can identify how you feel at the moment, and what thoughts are going through your mind. Surely, you can conclude that there's little chance that anyone cares about what you're buying. You may reason with yourself that pharmacists see hundreds of people daily, meaning that they most likely don't question people's medications or judge them for the illnesses they're treating. This will help discourage the physiological response pattern that happens at this time. The more you evaluate the rationality of your response, the more you train your mind against activating such intense mechanisms.

Cognitive restructuring, as one of the crucial components of both CBT and exposure treatment, involves the evaluation of the context of triggering situations. In terms of behavior, change has been proven to reduce numerous symptoms of social anxiety. Studies have shown that once the individual shows signs of improvement in their rationale, their neurological processes also changed. In fact, researchers detected a decrease in blood flow to the amygdala during public speaking, which suggests that the fear-inducing part of the brain is less stimulated. The changes were also detected in MRI imaging of the research subjects, which showed that the change was significant enough to provide a noticeable physical change in the way the brain works. In this study, participants were trained in certain cognitive techniques, and then the MRI images were recorded and compared to those who didn't have SAD, along with the previous scans of participants. This research showed that behavioral treatment led to a significant decrease in negative feelings. After behavior and exposure training, the participants showed an improved ability to use the right self-evaluation strategy and to reduce their emotional reactivity.

How to Prepare for Exposure

Engaging in the situations you fear helps you change the natural process of conditioning and reduces its weight. However, before creating a real-life situation, you need to prepare yourself thoroughly.

Create an Exposure Ladder

You will list and rank the situations you fear and that provoke anxiety. It is important to face the situations starting from the least fear-provoking to the most dreaded to keep the levels of anxiety to a tolerable level.

Start From the Bottom

First, you should work with the therapist to simulate situations you fear, starting from the bottom of the list. After that, you'll gradually approach the situations that your fear more. This can be done in real time situations, by using visualization techniques or role-play. Simulating these situations will help reduce anxiety over time.

Exposure is used by the majority of SAD treatments, particularly CBT. However, you should be fully open to the exercises so that they are effective. You need to pay full attention to the activities and experience them fully, allowing the symptoms to occur. It is important to avoid maladaptive defense mechanisms. You shouldn't try to protect yourself from fear by focusing attention on something else, because this lessens the effects of exposure. Aside from planning the exact activities, planning the details leading up to them, including what you'll do to get ready, will help you feel more secure and confident. Alone, or alongside your therapist, plan the following aspects of exposure. The exposure needs to be done in time intervals that allow you to get ready, practice, and take time to process the experience and reflect on it. Obviously, practicing live exposure before work might not be a good idea, because you should take time to rest and reflect afterward. If your activity involves other people, it's important to plan the interaction so that it fits the frames of being legal and appropriate. For example, if your mission is to ask someone out on a date, it's important to plan out the interactions so that it comes across as safe and appropriate. It's important to design situations that are challenging to you, but not inappropriate to the person who is participating. Mapping out what you want to say in advance, adjusting your schedule to leave enough time for exercise, and making sure you'll be fully prepared will help you feel better about yourself and to feel more confident.

Confront Feared Social Situations and Feelings

After careful planning, now is the time to experience the feared situation. The course of the situation is, by this time, already planned out, and now it's up to you to perform it well. Here are a couple of guidelines for successful exposure:

Practice Confident Body Language

People can unconsciously use body language that reflects their state of mind in reverse. However, you can also use your body language to make yourself feel more confident. Practicing confident body language will show you that you have more control over your emotions than you think. Based on your perception about how you should feel, your body creates neurotransmitters that create emotions and physiological responses, coordinating with feeling. If you're in a stressful environment, and you're always worried that you will have an unpleasant experience, your body will produce cortisol, a stress hormone, as well as adrenaline and other brain chemicals that fuel your fight-or-flight response. This is a very unhealthy mechanism if it becomes constant. Even if you're not in a stressful environment, you can start to experience this self-induced stress as you unconsciously perceive you need it. This way, your body reflects your inner feelings.

As a result of such a stressful state of mind, you may try to shy away, avoid eye contact, and live in fear of either a single or every social interaction. On the other hand, people who feel safe and confident tend to act and speak slowly. To do this, assume the postures and movements that tell your body to feel like you're safe. This means relax and stretch, extending your limbs and relaxing your shoulders.

Make sure to stand and sit with good posture, and slow down your movements. These poses will lower your cortisol and increase the "happy" neurotransmitters like serotonin and dopamine, which correspond with feeling good.

When you practice confident body language, you will learn to open your mind to the possibility that you can actually have a pleasant experience in social situations. However, this takes exercise and repetition. The more you practice, the better you will feel. However, you need to be patient and give yourself time.

Don't Avoid Social Situations

Despite feeling awkward, you must practice being in social situations as much as possible. Ideally, you will find social events and go by yourself. This way, you won't have a friend to stick around. That will reduce your fear of socializing. When you socialize by yourself, you practice coping with the awkward feelings that come your way. When you practice the confident body language, in this situation, maintaining eye contact, good posture, and speaking slowly, make sure to also focus on your breath. You should breathe slowly, deeply, and evenly.

While socializing, try not to focus on a specific goal, like going on a date or making new friends. Instead, make it your only goal to enjoy this time and feel good, focused on the fact that you are working to improve yourself your confidence and social skills. When you focus on an outcome, this will make you more nervous. When you come back home, try to reflect on your experiences positively and validate your good efforts.

Track Your Interactions

This isn't as strict as to write down every conversation you have, but keeping records of the interactions that you had the opportunity to avoid will help increase your confidence. This way, you will shift your focus from avoidance and social failure to social success. You can turn to this list when you need a boost of confidence to remind you that you have already made progress and you can make contact with others when you choose to stretch out of your comfort zone.

The more you practice, the more your confidence and self-esteem improve. Keep in mind that your goal isn't to impress anyone. Instead, the goal is to go through the experience and to make an interaction. Make your mind to have enjoyable conversations, regardless of how you feel.

Find Confident Role Models

It will be easier for you to learn confidence when you spend time with confident people. These people will become a positive influence that will help you build your social skills. Finding the right role models means focusing on spending time with people you appreciate and admire.

Resort to Mindfulness

Meditation is a proven method to help you relax, reduce anxiety, and become more self-aware. It helps treat social anxiety through practicing awareness of the present moment. You should meditate between 20 and 40 minutes daily, either at once or distributing the time to multiple, shorter sessions throughout the day. When meditating, you should be sitting either on the floor or in a chair, with your feet touching the floor, and palms of your hands facing down and touching either floor or your legs. Once you're comfortable, you can close your eyes and begin meditating:

- Take up to five deep breaths. Focus on the sensations that the breath creates as it travels through your body.

- After that, start counting your breaths. Count to three as you breathe in, hold your breath for three seconds, and count to three as you breathe out. Repeat between five and fifteen times, depending on the length of meditation.

- Allow random thoughts that are going through your mind to flow in and out of your consciousness, without engaging in rumination.

- Once you feel calm and ready to end the meditation, gently open your eyes.

This simple meditation helps you shift focus from obsessive thoughts to your body and environment and focus on the present moment. The more you practice present awareness, the easier it will be to resist rumination and negative thoughts.

Socialize as Often as You Can

Regularly socializing with different types of people will help you overcome social anxiety and boost confidence. There may be certain people that make you feel good, and there are those who trigger your insecurities. Don't avoid the people who trigger the insecurities, as it is a good opportunity to overcome your limitations. Talk to employees at shops or with anyone appropriate to communicate with randomly throughout the day.

Initiate Interactions and Social Events

Instead of waiting for someone to invite you on a date or to go out, be the person who will go out and initiate the interaction. Once you've learned how to cope with the fear of talking to people, and learned lessons about confident body language, try planning your own events. Think about the activities you find enjoyable, and would want to do with your friends. It could be anything from sitting together to playing sports. It's important to learn how to assume a leadership role and be the host(ess).

Express Yourself

Being constantly worried about rejection can limit your own self-expression. This way, you become inhibited, and you don't share your sense of humor, intelligence, compassion, and other positive traits. To learn to express yourself, it's good to start doing it when you're on your own, and practice speaking your mind when you're around other people. However, this doesn't mean that you have to act without a filter. It's alright to withhold things that you think might be hurtful to others or are inappropriate.

Learn How to Self-Entertain

Start spending quality time with yourself and practice talking, joking, and everything else you're insecure doing in social settings. Try recording yourself to affirm that you are doing well and that it's not embarrassing. This will help you be less self-conscious about your social performance.

Exposure therapy for social anxiety helps you overcome fears through facing situations. In terms of social anxiety, exposure is aimed at performance situations. Usually, exposure is trained and practice with the assistance of a licensed therapist as a part of CBT. However, you can use it in your daily life. Avoiding situations that trigger anxiety only feeds into the disorder, making you feel worse about it over time. In addition, leaving a situation while in a state of panic also increases the fear. Exposure is all about gradually introducing the situations that frighten you until you learn that you can survive, and it eventually subsides.

Workbook: Exposure Ladder Ideas

Here are some suggestions for designing exposure for different triggering situations:

- If you are afraid of eating in public, you may be afraid that you might embarrass yourself. Eating exposure therapy teaches you to learn how to eat in public by gradually starting to enjoy meals, starting from the situations that are intimidating to those that are unnerving.

- If you're afraid of using public restrooms, this can be an isolating state that causes you to stay home or to leave social events when you have to go to the bathroom.

- If you dread talking on the phone. This is easy to practice. For example, you can start by going through tomorrow's to-do list, and check if there are any calls you need to make. To reduce your anxiety, you can plan out the call and write down what you want to say, and how. Next, write it down and rate the types of calls from easy to hard, and start from the bottom of the list.

- Social situations are amongst the most feared in those who suffer from social anxiety. Usually, there is a hierarchy of frightening situations. Start by creating this hierarchy and writing down which particular situations are challenging for you. Usually, people are least afraid of small interactions like going to the store and most afraid of attending social events and public speaking. When practicing these types of exposures, you can plan out events to the detail to feel more secure. When planning for informal events, there's no particular task for you to do. You should plan out to relax and have fun.

- If you're afraid of being the center of attention, you can overcome this by laying out the situations that place you into the center of attention and cause different degrees of discomfort. For example, you may be least afraid around your closest friends and most afraid when you are speaking publicly in front of strangers. You can write down these types of situations and start from the bottom of the ladder by first giving a monologue in front of your group of friends, and then a group of coworkers, and then at a meeting.

- Fear of public speaking is usually one of the most intense concerns in social anxiety disorder. There are many opportunities for you to practice exposure to public speaking — one of them being sharing your video recordings on social media. If there's a speech you need to prepare, and you're dreadfully afraid of it, there are different ways to scale up exposure before the event, so that you can gain more confidence. For example, you can give a trial speech to your friends, then to your coworkers. By witnessing positive feedback, you will gradually become more confident in your abilities.

- Fear of conflict partially results from impaired self-esteem, but also from doubting your abilities to partake in discussions, even if you believe that you are right. Learning about assertive communication helps you solve conflicts by voicing your concerns in a peaceful way that helps another person understand you right.

Chapter 8: Treatment for Social Anxiety Disorder

Cognitive-behavioral treatment of social anxiety focuses on restructuring and changing the context of situations. It highlights the role of cognitive distortions and biases in the symptoms of the disorder. However, it is important to know that those with generalized anxiety tend to keep some of the symptoms after the treatment. This includes those whose avoidance strategies and fears are fixated on particular types of situations. Here, social skills training needs to be combined with Cognitive Behavioral Therapy to increase the chances of success. Social skills training teaches that anxiety has a lot to do with the reduction in social performance, which is only a reflection of a deficit in social skills and our capacity of social performance levels. The reduced social skills are thought to be connected with anxiety and avoidant and safety behaviors. The effects of these factors and impaired skills depend on each individual, which is why it's really hard to make an accurate assessment before looking into a person's individual condition. Social skills training uses interventions to correct the social skills deficits in those with SAD (Hope, 2004).

Why is Social Skills Training Important?

The training in social skills helps people with SAD process to express their feelings appropriately.

Anger Processing

People with SAD may express intense anger after receiving negative judgment or whenever they feel pressured to engage in triggering situations. New studies show that those with SAD tend to experience heightened irritation in cases without any direct provocation, and they also tend to express anger if criticized. They also believe less in the credibility of others and how much they can rely on them.

While some have problems with lower assertiveness, others have problems with hostility, anger, and mistrust in promises. This can come from the perceived negative judgment, where the anger is expressed in the threat of future negative judgment, whether it's real or perceived. Anger increases in the prospect of judgment and scrutiny, whether real or perceived, enhancing the anxiety, isolation, and other symptoms. While suppressing anger is uncomfortable, it is typical for those with SAD to show resentment and be very critical of others. This has been connected to their fear of negative judgment. However, people with SAD are more prone to suppressing anger. This also has negative effects. Suppressing anger tends to affect their quality of life and the effectiveness of their treatment more than those who don't have problems with suppressed anger. This study showed that those with suppressed anger also have a greater level of anxiety in expressing anger and greater levels of depression.

Those with greater levels of anger in response to negative judgment and those who suppressed anxiety and depression have a lower quality of life. They were prone to extreme angry outbursts. They have more frequent episodes, chronically felt frustrated, and feel like they are mistreated. They are more likely to suppress anger, which means they hold grudges and are highly critical of others. With the use of CBT, there was a recorded reduction in overall anger to received negative judgments, which took around 12 weeks to achieve. During this time, patients managed to identify the irrational beliefs associated with anger. They also became aware of the isolating effect that these patterns had on them, causing them to put distance between themselves and others, which is why anger is so often used as a defense mechanism.

Reduce Rumination and Re-evaluation

Those with SAD tend to have problems with emotional regulation and reactivity that result from irrational beliefs and assumptions, safety behaviors, and other types of avoidant behaviors and coping mechanisms. The process of rumination is one of these mechanisms, while the other is adaptive re-evaluation.

Rumination is a method of unproductive focus on your mood by recalling the consequences and symptoms of previous events. Rumination is also a significant component of depression. After a social event, those with SAD tend to focus on the negative aspects of themselves and the reactions from others that they have received. They compare their impressions with an unrealistic image of what they perceive to be desired. This increases the symptoms of anxiety over time. However, these memories are most often distorted and inaccurate. This way, rumination is strengthening and maintaining the irrational beliefs present in social anxiety.

Regain Rational Evaluation

Opposite to that, cognitive evaluation is an adaptive process of emotional regulation that reduces emotional reactivity, mental distress, and improves overall well-being. It is considered that re-evaluation is one of the most significant parts of cognitive restructuring. CBT uses techniques that reduce anxiety and distress when one faces intrusive automatic thoughts during triggering situations.

However, those with lower ability to use these strategies also have lower self-efficacy skills in using evaluation. Cognitive Behavioral Therapy increases the use of re-evaluation, which mediates self-efficacy and as a result reduces the symptoms of social anxiety. These improvements have been recorded to last even one year after treatment. Those who participated in this study had 16 weeks of the hourly weekly sessions, with 90 minutes of sessions that included exposure. These sessions included exercises, education, cognitive restructuring, exposure, the work on core beliefs, as well as consolidation treatment.

Emotional dysregulation was noted here, and rumination is used as a strategy to avoid facing one's emotions. What happened in this study was that participants focused on the signals to change the emotional response, but this happened without making a cognitive change. This can create a cycle of unproductive negative thoughts. Their interpretations of social events became increasingly unfavorable over time.

To help alter these patterns, re-evaluation was introduced. Re-evaluation is an important part of CBT. It is a process during which a person changes the way they think about social interactions and triggering situations, which in return helps them change the way they feel. It is considered to be a more adaptive (functional and better) strategy because it is a mechanism that a person uses to question different aspects of the situation. Rumination has, aside from an increase in social anxiety, other adverse effects, such as biased interpretations of events and biased memories.

Rumination happens before, during, and after the social events. Since the focus of the thought process is mainly negative and based on unrealistic standards, it affects the person in a way that distorts their interpretations and memories. Essentially, the more you ruminate, the less accurate your memories and recollections of the situations will be, and your self-evaluation will be more negative as a result.

Despite being increasingly negative, it is vital to remember that these evaluations are inaccurate and irrational. When you recall an event, make sure to consider the fact that the things you are remembering are most likely untrue and that there might be many inaccuracies in your view on the situation. Regardless of accuracy, recollecting situations also tend to cause severe emotional responses. Training, on the other hand, helps people forming more practical ways of thinking.

Cognitive Bias

Cognitive biases affect the accuracy of the evaluation of past events. The emotion regulation tactic that most people use is expressive suppression, which means suppressing one's own emotions. Cognitive re-valuation is a better alternative to that.

Judgment bias is distorted reasoning that happens in a social situation. It creates an exaggerated estimation of chances that the negative events will have major negative consequences. It appears that people with SAD tend to exaggerate the estimated effects that the situation can have on them. These perceptions strongly affect the intensity of symptoms. What this means is that when you exaggerate, you overestimate how you think the situation will affect or has affected you. This can increase your anxiety symptoms.

When people perceive events as less dangerous, it's easier to control the symptoms of social anxiety. It also relates to the reduction of fear in similar symptoms. There are also forms of judgment biases related to interactions and relationships, which improve with cognitive-behavioral treatment.

Emotional Regulation Exercises

Strategies for emotional regulation with SAD include exercises to correct the use of dysfunctional strategies for emotional regulation. Suppression of emotion is one of these strategies, and it increases with the perceived consequences of the negative event. This means that the more you are afraid, the more you are likely to suppress your feelings. Fear of rejection, for example, can lead to the suppression of feelings of need for a loving partner to avoid the perceived danger of hurt. This also increases anxiety and other negative feelings.

The use of cognitive evaluation strategies in social situations helps people learn to modify the interpretations of the events, their role in them, and the values they associate with these situations. This helps overcome behavioral avoidance and, overall, many of the dysfunctional coping mechanisms.

Avoidant behaviors are also linked to depression. Depression increases the negative effects and symptoms of distress. It also decreases positive emotions and satisfaction with life, a person's self-esteem, and increases the symptoms of depression and anxiety. Suppression and avoidance also cause people to feel a lot more uncomfortable in both negative and positive situations and can cause them to avoid forming relationships with others. In combination with cognitive-behavioral therapy and social skills, treatment improvements were recorded in the reduction of cognitive biases.

Improved Social Skills

Improving social skills can correct some of your behavioral deficits such as the lack of eye contact and conversation skills that not only create negative reactions in other people but also make you feel bad about yourself and increase your anxiety. It remains unclear whether social skills are a result of some developmental tendencies, such as the lack of developing social skills in childhood, or if they're a result of avoidance behaviors. The most likely answer is that poor social skills result from the influence of multiple factors combined. The lack of social skills is preventing you from spending quality time with people, and it is also making you look at yourself more negatively. Poor social skills are even thought to be behind failure at work, school, and relationships.

Social skills training for SAD includes behavioral modeling, corrective feedback, social reinforcement, and self-guided homework exercises. The more you repeat acting in certain situations you are afraid of, then you better learn how to manage them. There is also an exposure element to these exercises, and cognitive elements, such as receiving corrective feedback about how your behavior is adequate to the situation.

CBT Treatment Model for Social Anxiety

One of the first steps in your treatment will be to address the social standards you perceive to be accurate. Mainly, people with social anxiety disorder tend to view social norms as unrealistically high. They also believe that they are incompetent to fulfill these standards.

Set Goals

Every CBT treatment model starts with setting goals (Hope, 2004). When setting goals, you need to set social goals that are concrete, behavioral, and objective, because these goals are a way for you to evaluate your performance. One of the common goals is to learn how to assess your effectiveness rationally.

First, you will define your goals. For this, you will need to clarify social standards and expectations logically. After you successfully set your goals, you'll use them to evaluate your social performance. After that, you will define the right strategy to meet your goals. The goals must be realistic and adequate.

Think about the best ways to achieve your goal. This will steer your attention towards more rational demands of the situations rather than false impressions and behaviors. These goals can be very specific, and they don't have to be generalized to have a beneficial effect. For example, you can set a goal to ask someone what time it is.

After exposure has been practiced, you will evaluate the event based on whether or not you reached your goals regardless of whether or not anxiety was present. For example, if your goal was to ask someone on a date, the evaluation will be based on whether or not you did it and not how you felt in that situation.

Modify Attention

You only have a limited amount of attention, and you have limited abilities to focus your attention to multiple things at the same time. With SAD, you are focusing the majority of your attention inwards, to your self-evaluation, and not on the actual external activities. However, when you focus your attention inwards, you are neglecting to focus on exterior tasks. When this happens, you are more likely to make mistakes. Doing so only increases your anxiety, and it makes you perform with less productivity. People with SAD tend to focus on their sensations. Instead of thinking about their activities in the situation, they are thinking about how their heart is racing, how they are making a fool of themselves, how they feel like their head is dizzy, etc.

They are obsessed about whether or not their symptoms are noticeable. To overcome this habit, you need to be aware of how this lack of focus increases your anxiety, and train your mind to shift attention to performance tasks. You are to focus on the exterior rather than the interior. This is how you do this:

- First, stop focusing on your physical sensations.

- Next, start paying better attention to your physical environment. After that, try to focus on a specific topic for at least 30 seconds.

- Rate your anxiety levels from 0 to 10.

Improve Self-Image

People with SAD tend to feel uncomfortable looking at themselves in the mirror, pictures or videos, or when listening to their voice on audiotapes. What can be done to improve a person's self-perception is to confront them with a realistic image of themselves. This helps reduce self-criticism, build self-confidence, and improve self-image. There are multiple ways to do this, such as video feedback, audio feedback, mirror exposure, group feedback, and others. What's common for all these exercises is that you are first required to write down the impression of yourself and then evaluate how accurate this perception was. Usually, people have positive opinions of themselves when observing themselves at an audiotape or videotape, and they realize that their insecurities aren't as noticeable as they think they are. It is also useful for them to see that nobody else can tell their symptoms, like sweating, trembling, and others.

Exposure Treatment

Gradual exposure with CBT is done to reduce avoidance and safety behaviors. Usually, there are two types of actions common to social anxiety, such as low activity. Because anxiety drains so much of your physical energy, you become sluggish during everyday activities. This is also common across different types of anxiety and depression. Avoidance happens when you avoid situations out of fear. It is a common symptom of all forms of anxiety and depression. It happens in situations when you feel you can't cope with it. These behaviors are:

- Obvious avoidance, which is when you avoid particular situations, people or places

- Subtle avoidance and safety behaviors, which happens when you saddle actions for relief and to help cope with anxiety

When you avoid facing situations, you're unable to learn that these situations aren't bigger than you and that you can deal with them. They enhance your belief in being unable to manage and prevent you from learning that the symptoms won't harm you. Through gradual exposure, you are fighting against avoidance and gradually facing your fears. This helps you build your confidence slowly and convince yourself in your ability to cope with situations that used to be unbearable. When you confront fears, your fight-or-flight response gets triggered. However, if you persist through a situation and this fear, the anxiety starts going down. Each time you face it, the tension reduces even more. This is the so-called gradual desensitization that happens when your body and brain get used to experiencing social situations. The more you learn that nothing bad will come out of them, the more desensitized your body becomes to anxiety.

In these situations, you are testing your worries and whether or not your negative predictions will prove truthful. If you use safety and avoidance behaviors, you are unable to go through these experiences and ignore anxiety.

Exposure Tests

To practice exposure properly, it is important to do exposure tests first. Exposure tests serve to test whether or not being exposed to your predictions will have as negative of an outcome as you fear. Although you can predict your evaluations aren't accurate, the physical responses of anxiety won't reduce until you go through the experience.

Creating an exposure step ladder helps you identify different levels of anxiety that the various situations induce. While most people feel like there are certain situations they can't cope with, this isn't true. Each step you take helps you reassure yourself that you have enough strength and the ability to cope with the situations. It also helps you see that there are different degrees of anxiety and that you can change your responses and feelings by looking at the different expert aspects of the situation.

To start creating your exposure step ladder, you first need to write down your goals. The second step is to create a list of the social situations that trigger anxiety, while the third step is to rank them from lowest to highest. Exposure starts by picking a low-intensity task first.

You should write down your predictions about how the situation will go before performing the task and later reflect on the results of the events. There are multiple methods of cognitive-behavioral therapy used to treat social anxiety. Usually, the goals of the treatment are:

- To identify the irrational core beliefs that lie behind the fears

- To pinpoint the exact thought patterns

- To replace them with more balanced, realistic views

As the name suggests, CBT treatment consists of cognitive and behavioral exercises aimed to correct errors in judgment. Cognitive treatment helps you correct automatic thoughts, which, while highly unrealistic and inaccurate, holds a great amount of power over you. Changing the way you think through consistent repetition and practice over several months, helps you change your mindset.

CBT, on the other hand, also focuses on behavioral changes. Using techniques such as exposure, you learn to conquer your fears with care, gradually. Exposure needs to be a step-by-step process, and well structured to help you determine the right lessons.

Mindfulness Treatments for SAD

Mindfulness is a therapeutic approach that helps you focus and become self-aware by becoming presently aware of the moment. In terms of treatment of SAD, mindfulness enables you to be more aware of your behavior patterns. It helps you observe your actions from a more reasonable point of view. As a result, you can start responding in more practical ways. There are two ways in which cognitive-behavioral treatment applies mindfulness in treating SAD. These include Acceptance and Commitment Therapy (ACT) and Dialectical Behavior Therapy (DBT).

ACT helps you find the root cause of your suffering by helping you see how your behaviors reflect your evaluations, self-criticism, and automatic thoughts. While ACT doesn't aim to correct the symptoms of anxiety directly, it helps you accept who you are in the present moment, which in return helps reduce your symptoms.

DBT, on the other hand, helps you cope with stressful events by learning how to tolerate different types of unpleasantness. This therapy teaches you to accept the state of suffering by processing them without being overwhelmed. These techniques are different than cognitive-behavioral therapy. What they have in common is that they nurture self-awareness of your thoughts and behaviors. However, they have a different approach to the condition. CBT states that your thoughts cause anxiety, while ACT says that you struggle to deny the feelings that cause inner conflict and stress as a result.

Mindfulness Meditation

There is a lot of evidence to suggest that mindfulness helps recovery from SAD. Mindfulness is considered to be an effective supplemental treatment for this disorder. Mindfulness, in combination with behavioral and acceptance strategy, can have an impact on the condition and yield improvement. Experiential avoidance is one of the processes that can be interacted with mindfulness. When a person wants to detach from their sensations, thoughts, feelings, emotions, and memories, it can create an emotional blockage and increase the symptoms. Experiential avoidance seems to manifest in numerous ways in social anxiety disorder.

Acceptance means to accept and become aware of one's psychological experiences without using defense mechanisms, as they create unpleasant sensations and symptoms like shaking and sweating, as well as anxious thoughts.

The use of mindfulness-based stress reduction programs has been proven to reduce symptoms of depression, stress, and anxiety. This approach has been proven effective to decrease experiences of negative emotions, reduce the activity of the amygdala, and increase the activity of brain parts that are in charge of focus and attention. Mindfulness-based stress reduction includes several practices, such as formal and informal meditation, focusing attention on physical sensations, eating meditation, as well as monitoring experience. Informal medications include shifting attention to the present moment. These meditations enable a person to observe their own experiences, including sensations, mental images, memories, thoughts, and feelings. Two meditations have proven most effective.

The first is the focused attention, where your focus is placed on breathing. This is voluntary, the selective emphasis on the present moment while evaluating the quality of one's attention.

The second is open-monitoring, which means placing attention to the observation of the present moment while accepting any experiences that come your way. These meditations have been proven to reduce rumination and emotional responses. They were also helpful for reducing symptoms of stress and anxiety, correct irrational assumptions, improve functioning, self-regulation, and the conscious focus of attention.

In this chapter, you learned how to apply multiple effective techniques to battle SAD. First, you learned why social skills training is so critically important. Training your social skills enables you to manage your emotions and responses better, which can reduce safety and avoidant behaviors, rumination, and self-criticism. Here you also learned about exposure therapy and CBT and that you can practice exposure as an individual technique.

To be effective, exposure therapy needs to be carefully planned out and strategic. It needs to target your negative core beliefs and other crucial issues that relate to your anxiety. Next, exposure needs to be gradual and never beyond what you find bearable. The purpose of exposure is to strengthen and empower you, not overwhelm you with anxiety, and cause further damage to your image and self-esteem. When using CBT, you will start from cognitive restructuring and questioning your thought process, and then move to other techniques. While exposure aims to prove your abilities, CBT has a goal to challenge and change your beliefs. With this information, you now understand what needs to be done so that you finally recover from social anxiety. In the next chapter, I'll tell you more about taking care of yourself after you finish SAD treatment. Furthermore, we will go over how to maintain your recovery and ways to prevent relapse.

Chapter 9: Maintaining Your Improvement and Planning for the Future

In the previous chapter, you learned more about CBT treatments for social anxiety. CBT includes many different treatment plans and techniques that you can tailor to your own needs. Hopefully, you discovered those that are a good fit for you. In this chapter, you'll learn how to stay well after you're done with your SAD treatment. While you may be feeling well in the current moment, there's always a possibility of spiraling back into SAD. I'll explain why it is important to keep paying attention to your lifestyle and habits after you're done with treatment. You'll learn about the possibility of relapse, and what you can do to prevent it. In addition, you'll also learn about the exact strategies and steps to take to notice the warning signs, and how to keep challenging yourself and broaden your horizons.

How to Maintain Your Improvement

Despite making progress with your treatment, it is always possible to relapse. If you're not paying attention to nurture and support your recovery, old symptoms can come back. Facing relapse isn't something that permanently takes away your progress. However, there are things that you can do to prevent it. You want to do as much as possible to make the positive changes last. For these purposes, it's essential to distinguish between lapse and relapse.

Lapse

Going through a lapse means that you temporarily return to unhelpful habits, which is typical. Unpredictable life circumstances, stress, and bad mood can often make you turn to avoidance and isolation. A lapse can happen easily, but what's important is that you can bounce back and return to healthy habits. A slip can be a one-time occurrence that doesn't mean that you'll automatically go through full-blown SAD again. An example of a lapse is when you go through a significant failure, loss, or a life change, that makes you temporarily anxious. If you lose your job or break up with a partner, it's common for anyone to want to withdraw. However, if you're able to proceed with a healthy social life, there's no cause for concern. Even if your anxiety occasionally comes back, it won't be a problem as long as you apply the right strategies of coping, emotional processing, or rational self-evaluation.

Relapse

Relapse, on the other hand, is a bigger problem. It means the return of your old dysfunctional thinking patterns and behaviors. When you are in relapse, it means that you employ the same coping strategies as before you started treating SAD. You can start with a simple lapse, and eventually move into relapse. When you catch yourself lapsing, you should put effort into correcting your behaviors, or you can move in the direction of decline. The more you beat yourself up over making a single mistake, the more you'll be prone to making a relapse. The more you choose to follow the postulates of healthy, rational thinking, the better you'll maintain your recovery long-term. Maintaining your recovery means refraining from using ineffective coping strategies, even when it seems tempting. Here a couple of strategies to prevent relapse:

- First, you need to practice. Practice your cognitive-behavioral skills every day.

- Maintain the habit of tracking your thoughts and connecting them with associated feelings and behaviors. This will enable you to notice if you start using avoidant behaviors, suppressing feelings, or withdrawing due to fear of judgment.

- Stay aware of your triggers. The same triggering situations that cause anxiety may still be sensitive for you after you went through the treatment. Because of this, you want to pay attention to the warning signs that signal that your fear of social contact and social judgment are starting to overwhelm you.

- Make sure to create a list of common symptoms that signal the rise of your anxiety, including physical symptoms, stress, automatic thoughts, rumination habits, life changes, avoidance behaviors, etc.

Plan Future Challenges and Improvements

Even if you didn't have SAD, there is a possibility that stressful events or losses might shake your confidence and activate dormant insecurities. However, if you have a history of SAD, everyday struggles with life, such as a career change, relationship problems, starting a family, and others, can easily make you spiral back into a dysfunctional pattern of self-defeating rumination. The chances are that you'll face negative self-criticism long after your symptoms subside. However, with the skills to rationalize and self-evaluate correctly, you'll be able to bounce back and maintain a healthy, positive self-image. To maintain your recovery in the long run, create a plan of what you will do in case you notice that you're starting to relapse. Include the following prevention measures:

- Scheduling an appointment with your therapist
- Repeating exercises that you used to do
- Relaxing more, and so on
- Proceed with challenges

It is normal that the more you grow and change, the greater your challenges will be. Just because you've conquered fears that were previously frightening that doesn't mean that you won't encounter new fears. New concerns can form as you gain new experiences. It's even possible that old fears come back in new, unfamiliar situations when you haven't quite figured out how to evaluate your success. This can happen if you decide to start a family or receive a promotion at work. Stepping onto the newly-conquered territories also means getting used to new environments, relationships, and criteria. With a history of SAD, this calls for special attention to your social skills, coping skills, self-evaluation, and self-esteem.

Facing new fears is normal as long as you don't turn to avoidance, and process feelings with acceptance. A part of maintaining your recovery is to notice when you are up against them, and it's time to practice exposure.

Learn From Relapse

There's a lot of wisdom to draw from relapsing. Open up to learning from your early relapses, as they'll show you the "soft spots" in your mental structure. Lessons taught from regressions will teach you:

- What are the insecurities you're yet to overcome?

- What past traumatic events and experiences have left a lasting imprint on your emotional and mental structure, and are the hardest to overcome?

List Triggers

Whether or not you resort to old habits temporarily or for longer periods, you want to know how and why this happened and how you can prevent it in the future? For this, create a list of things that have upset you and caused a relapse. Note the degree and intensity of your anxiety, the actions you took, and your ability to evaluate the situation. You should be aware of which situations are still challenging for you, even though you were able to reduce your fears.

Last but not least, believe in your progress. If you went through correct CBT treatment, you possess the skills of coping with stressful events. If you get an episode or short relapse, that doesn't mean that your skills are completely gone. Perhaps you only need to practice a little bit more or to remind yourself of previous knowledge. Since negative self-criticism is one of the major dysfunctional thinking patterns in social anxiety, learn to be compassionate and care for yourself, and never beat yourself up for relapsing, as it only makes matters worse. Some of the most important aspects of preventing relapses include:

- Identifying the long term changes. You need to make in your lifestyles, such as with your work relationships and finances application of your learned skills.

- Changing your daily practices. After you identify a need for change, you also need to be aware of the limitations that you'll have to work around, such as behaviors and thoughts that you are prone to using that are unhelpful, like setting high, unrealistic goals.

- Identify what situations and people don't help your condition, such as contacting friends and family members who don't understand your condition, or being in a toxic environment.

- Monitor your lifestyle, habits, and health. This helps identify when you are sleep-deprived, unmotivated, or avoiding unpleasant situations and vulnerable to relapse. All of these are warning signs that you can track if you want to maintain your progress.

Keep Learning

There are many wide-available resources that can help you learn about SAD and coping skills. Try the following:

Books

"The Six Pillars of Self-Esteem: The Definitive Work on Self-Esteem by the Leading Pioneer in the Field" by Nathaniel Brandon gives you a practical, attainable, and realistic guide to build and maintain healthy self-esteem. In this book, the author presents you with a

detailed explanation of the concept of self-esteem, providing daily, weekly, and monthly exercises to build yourself up. This book is a must-read for anyone who struggles with anxiety and self-image.

"The Gifts of Imperfection: Let Go of Who You Think You're Supposed to Be and Embrace Who You Are" by Brené Brown is yet another simple-worded self-help book themed around self-acceptance and appreciating your own uniqueness. This book addresses perfectionism and shows you how to embrace your own limitations while offering a healthy, level-headed perspective on success and personal growth.

Online Videos

The Internet is flooded with experts in self-help who publish educational videos and tutorials on recovery from anxiety and other mental disorders. Beware of those who propagate positivity however, as a balanced mindset requires acceptance of inevitable hurt, pain, and unpleasantness. I recommend indulging in entertaining, yet highly informative work of Marissa Peer, Katie Morton, and The School of Life. These creators devote their time and work to put complex terms into plain language, and offer you simple, yet accurate and effective advice and coping strategies.

Congratulations! You've made it to the end of this book. I thank you for taking this journey with me. Hopefully, you now better understand yourself, your disorder, and what you need to do to get better. When I first started learning about SAD, I had numerous misconceptions about it. First, I thought my sister had Asperger's, and then I thought she might be bipolar. It wasn't until the end of our journeys with SAD, hers with recovery, and mine with research that I realized just how important it was to give yourself proper attention. I devoted the final chapter of this book to maintaining recovery, and for more than obvious reasons. More than tracking your progress and noticing that you're on a path to relapse, keeping track of your mind sends one strong message: You matter!

In its essence, childhood trauma is an experience of emotional distance that teaches you that you're unworthy and that you don't matter. As you grow, you generalize this lesson to believing that, no matter what you do, you're never good enough. Despite being untouched by the disorder, learning how and why my sister felt shook me to the core. There, I learned the importance of caring for those around me and always making sure that they feel accepted and appreciated. With this in mind, I make sure to ask, "*How are you doing?*" more than I like to talk about myself. Likewise, you're going to have to ask yourself, *"How are you doing?"* from time to time to stay well. Not just because of the history of SAD, but to show loyalty and devotion to yourself and honor the oath made to your inner child that you'll never reject them again as they were rejected once before.

DID YOU ENJOY THIS BOOK?

We would truly appreciate if you could leave a review on Amazon. We are an independent publishing company and read each and every review!

Conclusion

In this book, you learned how to recognize and treat social anxiety disorder and to show you practical strategies to cope with SAD and overcome it, using contemplation and exposure.

First, you learned that SAD is a mental disorder that is characterized by intense, overwhelming anxiety associated with either specific social interactions or social interactions in general. Then, you learned that this condition originates in childhood, with a possibility of genetic causes. This book also showed you that there are specific physiological traits and brain structure associated with SAD, which is an overactive amygdala with a prefrontal cortex that stimulates the gland, instead of calming it down. The devastating impact SAD can have on a person's life is more than apparent to anyone willing to look into it.

Using techniques like cognitive restructuring and graded exposure, with the most effective treatment being cognitive-behavioral therapy you can overcome shyness and SAD. It is so important for you to examine your anxious thoughts so that you can discover the beliefs that lie beneath them. This is because your thoughts mainly come from the beliefs that are inaccurate and make you think that there are dangers to certain situations that aren't true. This could cause you to make negative predictions about what can happen in certain situations while your entire thinking process is biased and leaning towards the negative. Indeed, SAD and profoundly negative core beliefs could shape your thinking as to see all the negatives about yourself and completely disregard the positives.

Cognitive restructuring is a process that teaches you to spot these thoughts and trace them before, during, and after the event. This will allow you to evaluate the accuracy of the automatic thoughts and perceived danger. For this, you must use the so-called Socratic approach and behavioral experiments. Based on your findings, you will be able to rationalize the thoughts and create rational alternatives that lean towards the positivity and balance.

Don't forget about the power of exposure. While exposure helps you conquer your fears and witness your strength and ability to survive, it's not the main point of the treatment. The focus of your recovery from SAD should be on spotting the irrationality behind your thoughts and correcting them. The most important thing is for you to understand that you are exaggerating the perceived risk of the situation.

To change, you must correct your dysfunctional thinking. There are four steps to do this. The first is to identify automatic thoughts or negative thinking patterns related to social events. The second is to identify the cognitive distortions, and the third is to use the Socratic dialogue to analyze your thought process rationally. The ultimate step is to form functional and rational thoughts based on reasonable criteria. Cognitive restructuring is used alongside other CBT techniques, role-play, exposure, group therapy, and written homework. These exercises are supervised by a therapist, with a considerable amount of work being done as homework.

You need to go through the situations that are upsetting you, to be able to challenge and defeat negative core beliefs. With this experience, cognitive restructuring is then used to identify, evaluate, and challenge the thought process that corresponds with your anxiety. Real-life exposure and independent cognitive restructuring are essential parts of treatment, as they teach you to challenge your fears and improve your self-esteem through experiences that prove your value. This way, you are able to better identify irrational beliefs and debunk them. You also learned that irrational beliefs have a key role in causing and maintaining the disorder. This happens because these irrational beliefs have the strength that can overwhelm and overpower one's person's rationality. Core beliefs refer to everything we believe about the world, and so their strength can be bigger than that of a fact. As challenging core beliefs can leave you feeling lost and confused, you learned the importance of making your exposures gradual, patient, gentle, and well-planned. I urge you not to try facing distressing situations ahead of time, as this can only be counterproductive. As we learned towards the end of this book, negative experiences can additionally enforce the negative self-image and worsen already low self-esteem.

Through this book, you also learned how vital self-esteem is for recovery from SAD. There's a reason why your self-esteem is low, the most common causes being childhood trauma and neglect, as well as unpleasant experiences and bullying. Low-self esteem develops out of negative core beliefs and that it could impair your life significantly. It is the low self-esteem that caused you to either isolate or self-sabotage through avoidance and purposeful failure. Although it may be hard to hear, low-self esteem is constantly seeking confirmation. If you don't value yourself enough, you'll always aim to prove yourself wrong.

On the other hand, if you choose to work on your self-esteem, that means that you'll have to face the worst things you believe about yourself, and oppose them with beliefs about yourself that you adore, appreciate, and value. I encourage you to be careful to notice and acknowledge all of your good sides. Negative self-criticism is always on the lookout to beat you down, and you want to oppose it with proof.

Hopefully, I have provided you with enough information to start recovering from SAD. I want to leave you with a final message, which is to commit to accepting and appreciating yourself for who you are in reasonable, leveled, and balanced ways. Irrational negativity can't be treated with irrational positivity, so make sure to stay away from any teachings that convince you that you can solve your problems with just "being positive." Mental stability doesn't mean facing a single negative emotion, it means accepting, acknowledging, and processing so it becomes a tool in your arsenal of self-awareness.

References

Antony, M. M., & Swinson, R. P. (2000). The shyness & social anxiety workbook: Proven techniques for overcoming your fears. New Harbinger Publications.

Barrera, T. L., & Norton, P. J. (2009). Quality of life impairment in generalized anxiety disorder, social phobia, and panic disorder. Journal of anxiety disorders, 23(8), 1086-1090.

Bruce, T. J., & Saeed, S. A. (1999). Social anxiety disorder: a common, underrecognized mental disorder. American Family Physician, 60, 2311-2328.

Causes of Social Anxiety. N.d. Retrieved from https://www.bridgestorecovery.com/social-anxiety/causes-social-anxiety/

Cath, D. C., Ran, N., Smit, J. H., Van Balkom, A. J., & Comijs, H. C. (2008). Symptom overlap between autism spectrum disorder, generalized social anxiety disorder and obsessive-compulsive disorder in adults: a preliminary case-controlled study. Psychopathology, 41(2), 101-110.

Children and shyness. n. d. Retrieved from https://www.betterhealth.vic.gov.au/health/HealthyLiving/shyness-and-children

Hirshfeld-Becker, D. R., Biederman, J., Henin, A., Faraone, S. V., Davis, S., Harrington, K., & Rosenbaum, J. F. (2007). Behavioral inhibition in preschool children at risk is a specific predictor of middle childhood social anxiety: A five-year follow-up. Journal of Developmental & Behavioral Pediatrics, 28(3), 225-233.

Hope, D. A., Heimberg, R. G., & Juster, H. A. (2004). Managing social anxiety: A cognitive-behavioral therapy approach client workbook. Graywind Publications.

Kashdan, T. B., Volkmann, J. R., Breen, W. E., & Han, S. (2007). Social anxiety and romantic relationships: The costs and benefits of negative emotion expression are context-dependent. Journal of Anxiety Disorders, 21(4), 475-492.

Kashdan, T. B., & Herbert, J. D. (2001). Social anxiety disorder in childhood and adolescence: Current status and future directions. Clinical Child and Family Psychology Review, 4(1), 37-61.

Olatunji, B. O., Cisler, J. M., & Tolin, D. F. (2007). Quality of life in the anxiety disorders: a meta-analytic review. Clinical psychology review, 27(5), 572-581.

Pickhardt, C. E. (2011). Adolescence and shyness. Retrieved from https://www.psychologytoday.com/us/blog/surviving-your-childs-adolescence/201106/adolescence-and-shyness

Rapee, R. M., & Heimberg, R. G. (1997). A cognitive-behavioral model of anxiety in social phobia. Behavior research and therapy, 35(8), 741-756.

Stein, M. B., & Stein, D. J. (2008). Social anxiety disorder. The lancet, 371(9618), 1115-1125.

Schneier, F. R. (2006). Social anxiety disorder. New England Journal of Medicine, 355(10), 1029-1036.

Stein, M. B., Fuetsch, M., Müller, N., Höfler, M., Lieb, R., & Wittchen, H. U. (2001). Social anxiety disorder and the risk of depression: a prospective community study of adolescents and young adults. Archives of general psychiatry, 58(3), 251-256.

Richards, T. N.d. What is Social Anxiety Disorder? Symptoms, Treatment, Prevalence, Medications, Insight, Prognosis. Retrieved from https://socialphobia.org/social-anxiety-disorder-definition-symptoms-treatment-therapy-medications-insight-prognosis

Cognitive Behavioral Therapy

Retrain your brain to overcome depression, anxiety, and panic attacks with CBT

12 Easy strategies made to find happiness and freedom

Written by:
George B. Wells

Table of Contents

Introduction **175**
Chapter 1 - Cognitive Behavioral Therapy (CBT) ..**180**
    What is Cognitive Behavioral Therapy? 180
    The History of CBT 181
    Understanding CBT 187
    What is CBT for? 188
    How can CBT help me and why? 189
    Why is CBT an Effective Therapy? 190

Chapter 2 - The Basics of CBT **192**
    What is the CBT Process? 192
    What are the basic principles of CBT treatment? 194
    What are Automatic Thoughts? 195
    What are Intrusive Thoughts? 196
    Automatic Thought Patterns 196
    Our Rules and Assumptions 197

Chapter 3 - Applications for CBT **199**
    Anxiety and Panic Attacks 199
    Phobias, PTSD and OCD 202
    Depression 204
    Anger Management 206
    Is CBT an Effective Treatment for Children and
    Adolescents? 207

Chapter 4 - What's my Problem? **210**
    Strategy 1 – Identifying your irrational and negative thinking
    patterns and actions with Journaling 211

What are Cognitive Distortions? 213
Defining Cognitive Distortions 213
Strategy 2 – Identifying and Making Sense of Cognitive
Distortions 219

Chapter 5 - Going Deeper into your Problems....223

Strategy 3 – Identifying, Assessing and Challenging Bodily
Reactions 223
Strategy 4 – Accessing Problem Causes Using the ABC Model.....229
Define Problems 233

Chapter 6 - Identify and Challenge your Core Beliefs 236

Mistakes 236
Strategy 5 - Self-Acceptance 238
Core Beliefs..240
Facing Problems, Assumptions and Beliefs Head-on 244
Strategy 6 - Exposure Planning 245
Understanding your Assumptions and Beliefs 247
Strategy 7 - Directly Targeting your Negative Core Beliefs 249

Chapter 7 - Relax, Regroup, and Believe 253

Strategy 8 - Relaxed breathing techniques 253
Move Beliefs from your Intellect to your Essence 257
Negativity versus Creativity 258
Strategy 9 - Muscle relaxation 259
Turn your Negativity into Creativity 261

Chapter 8 - Goal Setting for the Greater Good ...265

Problem Focused and Goal Orientated 265
Strategy 10 – Positive Prediction Planning 267
Strategy 11 - Finding your Focus 269

    How to set Effective Goals 272

    Top 3 Tips for Goal Setting 274

    Strategy 12 – Targeting your Triggers 277

Chapter 9 - Other CBT Techniques 281

    Assertiveness in CBT 281

    Five Top Tips to increase your Assertiveness 283

    Awareness Training 285

Chapter 10 - Mindfulness Based Cognitive Therapy (MBCT) 290

    Mindfulness Based Cognitive Therapy Versus Cognitive Behavioral Therapy 290

    Important ideas in Mindfulness-based Cognitive Therapy 292

    How does MBCT Work? 292

    Problems that may be addressed by MBCT 293

    MBCT Techniques and Exercises 294

    Benefits of Mindfulness 297

    Mindfulness Skills 297

    Other Alternative Cognitive Behavioral Approaches 298

Chapter 11 - CBT Treatment 301

    How will I know if CBT is for me? 301

    Do I need a Therapist? 303

    What Should I Expect on my First Visit with a CBT Therapist? ... 304

    What happens in a CBT Session? 305

    How Long does CBT Last and How Frequent are the Sessions? 307

    How do I Find the Right CBT Therapist for me? 307

    Why do I Need to have a Good, Collaborative, Therapeutic Relationship with my Therapist? 309

    Will the CBT Therapist be able to Understand and Appreciate

my own Background? 310
What about Medications? 312

Chapter 12 - Maintenance **313**
How to Maintain Automatic Thoughts and Cognitive
Distortions 314
Find the Full and Objective Perspective 315
Emotional Reasoning 316
Forging a New Synapses 316
Avoiding Backsliding 316
Keep up CBT 317
How your New Health Brain Functions 318

Chapter 13 - BONUS CHAPTER: Ten Ways that CBT Techniques can be Used to Boost your Energy **320**
Conclusion **327**
CBT Workbook **329**
Reference List **378**

Introduction

"There are three musts that hold us back: I must do well. You must treat me well. And the world must be easy.
Ellis, A. (Brainyquote.com, 2019) [1]*"*

Life can be hectic and busy. It's not always easy to relax or take a moment to ourselves when we constantly live, work and breathe in pressurized environments. On a daily basis we deal with situations that affect us both mentally and physically so it's natural for us to feel overwhelmed as a result. Sometimes we want to escape but we can't exactly escape our mind, *so what can we do?*

The mind is complex as we don't always control our thoughts and how we feel. Stress is common, in fact it's probably more common than you think. It's everywhere and it deprives us of life's little pleasures because if we're stressed, it's hard to enjoy anything. Self-care can help us to lower our stress levels, but this is something that we barely make time for. *Sound familiar?*

We've all been there! Yet, self-care is often underrated. It's so important because the strain can become too much and this can lead to anxiety, depression, panic attacks, and intrusive thoughts as all the negativity we feel bears weight on our shoulders. The most important thing we can do in this situation is to acknowledge the struggles we face and that's not always easy. People often choose to ignore their problems, but ignorance is not bliss for long, because we can't ignore them forever. They build inside and increase with intensity, and this makes us miserable. Unhappiness can affect our mind and it slowly creeps out. The way we appear and behave starts to reflect this.

On occasion, we need a little help in order to work things out and improve our mental health. That's okay, people should always get help if they need it but again, we arrive at the very first step of dealing with a problem, and that's acknowledgement and acceptance. Once we acknowledge that we have a problem and accept that we need to do something about it, we can start considering solutions. We may need help from a therapist, especially in the beginning as this can really help us to identify what exactly it is that's affecting us. This isn't always a long-term solution as we may need to learn how to maintain our mental health. *Wouldn't it be great if we had the tools and skills we need to help and maintain our mental health?* Well you can! It's time to act and overcome these issues before they take hold and we can do this with Cognitive Behavioral Therapy.

If you want to make positive changes in your life because of how you feel, and you're not sure how, this book is for you. That means you've accepted that something must change in your life, and that's a positive step. If you're ready to review your feelings and behavior, address the problems in your life, and develop strategies and coping techniques that improve your state of mind then you've come to the right place.

Cognitive Behavioral Therapy (CBT) is designed to help you address the negative patterns in your life. It's a structured and systematic approach of looking at and dealing with pessimistic beliefs and behaviors that impact your life. CBT can have long-term benefits as it is an efficient, effective and long-lasting treatment for many psychological problems.

This book gives you a comprehensive introduction to CBT, but it will also help you to develop workable techniques that you can adopt into your life. It explores the different approaches and types of therapies on offer and will encourage you to question the assumptions you have on autopilot in relation to yourself and other people. CBT generally concentrates on the present but with knowledge and practice, it can also change the way you feel about your past and it can help you escape from the negative thinking patterns that haunt your mind. With your newly found freedom and flexibility, you will no longer be held back and can start looking forward to the future.

In order to become happier and improve your mindset, you must be open-minded when reading this book and willing to try the skills and methods suggested. You may find that you need a Cognitive Behavioral Therapist to help you identify and make the changes but if you are susceptible to the change, this simple shift in how we think and what we believe has so many benefits. Be careful not to confuse the word simple, with easy. CBT methods take time and practice, although it can be very enlightening.

CBT is a lifestyle change because it challenges the way you think, and thinking is an automatic brain function. It can give you back control and if you commit yourself you will reap the rewards. It's time to take charge of your own destiny, so now I ask you; *do you choose to stay stagnant, or will you embrace this possibly life-changing experience?*

Cognitive Behavioral Therapy is not a magic formula, but more a way of life that you can adopt into your routine to help you to rationalize and make sense of your thoughts and feelings, before they get out of control. In chapter 1, you will get your first taste of CBT (if you're not already familiar) as we'll explore what CBT is, how it was developed and how it can help us. As we move through the chapters, we will discover the principles of CBT, why this type of therapy works, and we'll look at CBT in depth by exploring its core beliefs and how we can apply this to our own individual situation. Be prepared, as CBT will push you to a whole new level as we look at goal setting and problem solving, possible treatments and practice, before we look at to mindfulness practices.

This book aims to inspire you by giving you the whole picture and towards the end of this book, we cover one of the most important parts of CET, maintenance. As mentioned earlier, this is a lifestyle change so it's important to nurture and maintain a healthy state of mind. If you want to find out how to do that, then you should certainly read this book.

Remember, CBT leads to a happy life!

Chapter 1 - Cognitive Behavioral Therapy (CBT)

So, what is cognitive behavioral therapy? If you're not already familiar with CBT, this question will certainly be in your mind right now. We already know that behavior is the way we act, and cognitive is to do with the mind, *but what do we really mean when we refer to Cognitive Behavioral Therapy?* You're about to find out because we're going to review this therapy and find out what it is exactly. We are going to go back to the roots of CBT, look at its history and discuss key theorists that developed CBT. This will help you to gain a stronger understanding of this topic, so we can find out how and why it can help you.

What is Cognitive Behavioral Therapy (CBT)?

Cognitive Behavioral Therapy is a kind of therapy that helps you alter your beliefs, as well as the way you behave and think. Mental health charity, Mind, suggests that this is a kind of talking treatment that teaches you important coping skills. They say that we can suffer negative emotions if we interpret a situation badly. They then suggest that we react and behave in a particular way because of this negative attitude (Mind, 2019).[2]

CBT in itself works to break this cycle. It helps you to change those negative thought patterns and focus on your current problems. It looks for ways to alter your state of mind every day, and this way it becomes part of your routine until you change your beliefs and attitudes. Of course, you have to work at this by using a range of CBT tools, skills and methods. CBT incorporates effective coping strategies that help with depression and anxiety related conditions, though it is not limited to these.

Dobson and Dozios (2010), claim that Cognitive Behavioral Therapies share three fundamental propositions at their core and they include the ideas that "cognitive activity affects behavior, cognitive activity may be monitored and altered, and desired behavior change may be effected through cognitive change."(Dobson, 2010, p.4.)[3]

Throughout this chapter, we are going to find out more about CBT, so that you have a stronger understanding of this. We will think about what t is and how it can help us.

The History of CBT

Cognitive Behavioral Therapy has been practiced much longer than most people probably think, as over the last few years this has increased its popularity and become better known. As CBT is both cognitive therapy and behavior therapy combined, it focuses on three key areas: how we think, feel and behave. *Simply Psychology* state that Cognitive Behavioral Therapy is "an umbrella term for many different therapies that share some common elements" and that's very true. The therapy itself can treat a wide variety of problems because it works on those three key areas, and ensures improvements are made across the board. Although Cognitive Behavioral Therapy itself was practiced in the mid 1950's and early 1960's, it began much earlier as psychologists and psychotherapists developed and theorized their practices over this period (McLeod, 2019).[4]

One of the earliest therapies in CBT was Rational Emotive Behavior Therapy (REBT), and this was developed in the 1950's by psychotherapist, Albert Ellis. He was the first to confirm that in order to help a person be happy with others, they have to be happy with themselves. After becoming increasingly unhappy with the psychoanalytic approach. He then began experimenting and researching Greek and Roman Stoic philosophers and their work. These Ancient philosophers suggested that most people are not troubled by things, as it is actually their own beliefs and attitudes towards those things that causes the issue (Ellis and Dryden, 1997).[5] This idea formed the basis for REBT and is essentially how this therapy was born.

Rational Emotive Behavior Therapy focuses on emotional and behavioral problems. The therapy aims to help a person address their unreasonable beliefs and transform them, so that they become reasonable. The first step to REBT is identifying the beliefs that hold a person back and then it encourages them to challenge these ineffective and often untrue beliefs by reflecting and testing reality (McLeod, 2019).[6]

Albert Ellis's REBT theory concentrated on something he called **common irrational assumptions** and basically, they are referencing the ideas we hold in relation to ourselves.

According to McLeod (2019), in *Simply Psychology,* they are:
1. They believe that they should be competent at everything.
2. When things don't go their way, they view it as being a catastrophic event.
3. They feel that they have no control over their feelings or happiness.
4. They feel that they need someone to depend on and that person should be stronger than them.
5. They are defined by their past history and this influences their life right now.
6. They consider it disastrous if they can't find the perfect solution to their problem because they believe that perfect solutions exist. [7]

Ellis believes that if we can change these assumptions by altering our thinking patterns by following something that he called *The ABC Model*. This 3-column model is still used today to assess the changes that need to be made in beliefs, attitudes and thinking patterns and we discuss this in chapter 5.

Another instrumental figure in CBT is Aaron Beck. Beck is responsible for developing Cognitive Therapy in the late 1960's. His approach was more commonly used as therapy for depression and the therapist's aim is to help clients recognize how their negative thoughts can be destructive and can ultimately be responsible for their depressive state. According to *Simply Psychology,* Beck believed "That a person's reaction to specific upsetting thoughts may contribute to abnormality." (McLeod, 2019). He goes onto discuss how confronting our issues is often upsetting but it can also be comforting. Beck calls these "automatic thoughts" and again, this is down to think patterns, and how a person's negativity can cause depression. Therapists who use this method, often challenge these thoughts by getting their client to apply different ways of thinking or interpreting their thoughts and feelings.[8] Beck (1967), highlighted three mechanisms that he considers to be the main causes of depression. He developed the cognitive triad which demonstrates the negative views we have of ourselves, the world and future. Beck also thought that negative self-schemas, often developed in childhood, usually follow a traumatic event. They develop a negative attitude and are often very cynical as a result. The third cause of depression is a result of errors in logic. He calls these 'Cognitive Distortions' and considers them to be a form of illogical thinking. We talk in depth about cognitive distortions in chapter 4. Negative thought patterns and attitudes often leave people feeling defeated. This can ultimately lead to feelings of anxiety, stress and depression. It can also start off panic and feelings of anxiety.[9]

Again, Beck's aim was to change these thinking patterns and help people stray from negative thinking, by taking a different view or approach. His method of therapy focused on the client finding their own solution, through guidance from their therapist. It's only when we consider cognitive therapy and REBT together, that we can really start to understand CBT. Combining the two therapies certainly made sense and has proved effective over the years.

Behavioral Therapy roots go back to the early 1900's when papers were produced by Skinner, Pavlov and Watson. It wasn't until the 1940's when this type of therapy became popular mental disorders, due to the effects of war. Alfred Adler's focus on how basic mistakes being the cause of negative emotions in the early 1900's, inspired Albert Ellis's REBT. Adler is said to be one of the earliest psychotherapists to recognize cognition as a part of psychotherapy (Klear Minds, 2015)[10].

Cognitive Therapy and REBT combined started off the Cognitive Behavioral Therapy movement in the 1950's and 1960's yet no texts existed until the 1970s. Dobson (2010, p.4.) reflects on the work of Mahoney, who had claimed to have "undergone a 'cognitive revolution' in the 1960's" but following that, the focus continued on clinical psychology when considering theories. There were a number of models created for CBT but over time, they were developed.[11]

The combination of the two made sense because behavioral therapies like REBT, often addressed neurotic conditions that influenced behavior but did not conquer depression. Cognitive therapies involve talking. They are client-led and involve a certain amount of self-discovery or realization that includes identifying those unhelpful beliefs, then challenging them and modifying our behavior and thinking patterns. On the other hand, REBT is very confrontational as the therapist can point out the problems. The methods used in REBT often depend on the person as an individual, but the methods chosen in cognitive therapy are often focused on the specific condition.[12]

Understanding CBT

We have discussed the roots of CBT so by now, you should be gaining an understanding of Cognitive Behavioral Therapy. We have also discussed Cognitive Therapy and Behavioral Therapy as separate and merged entities, but in order to understand CBT, it is important to start with a good definition. Once we understand the basic concepts that form this therapy, the more likely we are to understand the mechanics and then, we can build on this to build a more in depth understanding.

Klear Minds (2015) give an excellent explanation of CBT:
> *CBT explores the relationship between feelings, thoughts, and behaviours. As such, it arose from two very distinct schools of psychology: behaviourism and cognitive therapy. It's roots can be traced in these two models and their subsequent merging. (Klear Minds, 2015)*

It's obvious that CBT looks at the way we think, feel and behave because they are all linked together and disturbance in one, can influence another. For example, we are upset or angry, this will impact how we think and how we act. By using CBT approaches, all aspects are covered, and this is why this therapy is so successful. Merging cognitive and behavioral therapies was the real breakthrough in Cognitive Behavioral Therapy. As we move on to the different chapters in this book, we can start to enhance our understanding by exploring the different approaches and applying them. We now have a better understanding of CBT, so we can start to think about what it is actively used for.

What is CBT for?

CBT is used across the world to treat many health issues. In America, there are many private CBT professionals, and some counsellors and psychotherapists specialize in this as it's known to be an effective treatment method, especially for anxiety disorders and depression. Many people have a CBT therapist to help them and doctors are usually happy to refer on private clients for such therapy to help their patient, often before medication is prescribed, or to work alongside them. In the United Kingdom, it is actually promoted by the National Health Service (NHS) and they suggest that it is an effective and efficient way of treating many different mental health conditions. This includes depression, anxiety disorders, bipolar disorders, psychosis, borderline personality disorders, sleep problems and insomnia, panic disorders, anorexia, bulimia, phobias, obsessive consultant disorder, phobias, post-traumatic stress disorder, and also problems that relate to substance misuse. They also sometimes recommend CBT as a form of treatment for long-term health conditions like fibromyalgia, irritable bowel syndrome, and chronic fatigue syndrome. Obviously, this is not to suggest that CBT is always suitable for such conditions, but it has been known to help sufferers cope better with their symptoms (NHS UK, 2019).[13] CBT is now a recognized, well-researched and popular treatment, all over the world.

This list is not limited solely to these illnesses either, as on occasion, the treatment could be recommended for some other reason. Regardless, of what you use CBT for, there are certainly benefits for everyone. It can generally help you adopt a healthy mindset and become more mindful in your approaches to life.

How can CBT help me and why?

CBT can help you by challenging any beliefs, ideas, thinking patterns and behaviors that trouble you and cause difficulties. It helps you adopt a more open approach in which you can be honest with yourself. Sometimes in life we just have to let out how we feel and as this kind of therapy is recognized as a talking therapy, you can certainly do that.

With CBT you can work with a therapist or by yourself to identify these and then you focus on methods to change you in the future. It helps you to think in a more rational way and this can help you to alter the way you feel. CBT focuses on what's going on right now, but sometimes you can review your past and think about how the past has influenced the way you think and behave. It is not a quick fix, but you will discover new approaches, and use different methods that enable you to stop the cycle of negative thinking and behavior. Even if you sometimes revert to feeling to your old patterns, you will be able to stop and take a moment to reflect due to your newly found awareness. You will have the tools, skills and strategies you need to cope with your feelings and thoughts, which will ultimately alter your behavior (Mind, 2019)[14].

Why is CBT an Effective Therapy?

CBT is an effective therapy because of its personalized approach. It is problem-focused and goal-oriented when it comes to finding a solution, and it encourages you to learn proven strategies and skills to overcome and cope with problems in the long-term.

Think of CBT techniques as being your toolkit. You are given a range of tools to fix something, and it's up to you which one you choose. If it doesn't work, you can choose another. Cognitive Behavioral Therapy can help with many different problems because it addresses three things: thoughts, emotions and actions. These three things often work hand in hand because if we think of something, it can cause us to feel a specific way and act a specific way. CBT gets to the bottom of the whole problem because it's an all-rounded approach that attempts to change the way you think, assess your emotions and consider how you act, before you actually do anything automatically. It's a life skill that can help you lead a happy, positive and rational life.

Chapter 2 - The Basics of CBT

If you've made it to chapter 2, you must think that CBT sounds amazing and you're right but in order to start treatment, you need to know the basics. We all have to start somewhere, so don't worry if you are still getting to grips with CBT. Bobby Davro once said, "The measure of success is happiness and peace of mind." (Davro, 2019)[15] but happiness and peace of mind can also lead to your success as it's only with a clear mind, that we can start to truly seek out what we want in life.

It's time to explore the basics of CBT by discussing the CBT process, ideas and principles. Once we know what's causing our negative thoughts and behaviors, we can focus on CBT as a goal-orientated, problem-solving therapy. In order to understand Cognitive Behavioral Therapy and how we can use it, we first need to know the basic principles.

What is the CBT Process?

If you want to start with CBT, you need to know how it works. There is a very simple process, and the diagram below will help you understand how CBT can encourage you to identify and solve your problems.

You have a problem!
You might know you have a problem, but you might not be able to put your finger on what it is exactly. You turn to CBT to figure this out or solve it.

Identify your Problem
CBT will then encourage you to figure out what your problems are exactly and analyze those.

Set your Goals
Goal setting is an important part of CBT. Once you know your problems you can start to set goals by considering what your problems are right now, and what your ideal is. *What do you want?*

Problem Solving Time
Now you know what your problems are, it's time to dig deeper. Sure, CBT focuses on the now, but you need to work on your core beliefs, so that you can work on long-term change.

Apply the Techniques
When you're at the stage, you are really trying to make a difference. You're addressing your problems, aiming for your goals and changing your whole mindset. Keep trying and applying CBT until you achieve your goals.

Practice and Maintenance
It's important to build CBT methods into your daily life so that they become normal. There are several CBT techniques to try to build on, and you should maintain CBT to ensure you don't fall into repeating thought and behavior patterns.

What are the Basic Principles of CBT treatment?

We have discussed what CBT is already, but what are the basic principles? Well, in order to understand this, we need to think about the different concepts. Cognitive Behavioral Therapy is a type of psychotherapy that helps you change your automatic thought patterns, cope with your emotions, and challenge your negative behaviors. *Has anyone ever told you that your actions have consequences?* Well, they do! The way we react can stop us from moving on our lives, and that is why it is so important.

The basic principles of Cognitive Behavioral Therapy, lies within its name:

Cognitive = This is because the whole idea of CBT focuses on our ideas, beliefs, thoughts and generally how we feel.

Behavioral = You already know that behavior is something we do, or the way we act. Sometimes this can be driven by how we feel or our emotions.

Therapy = If we are in therapy, we are receiving treatment for something we have, are trying to work out, or fix it. The therapy eventually remedies the problem.

Think about an occasion when you've been reactionary. Maybe this is because someone takes something for you or treats you badly. We can be reactionary as our thoughts or behaviors are automatic, and as a result as we struggle to control our gut-reaction. This means we can't always help the way we feel or act, so we get emotional and behave without thinking. This is because we are programmed to think or react in a negative way instantly.

These basic principles indicate how this therapy is focused on what you think and how you act in relation to an event or trauma. They are like a gut-reaction as we respond without thinking. Our thoughts and behaviors occur regularly, *but what are automatic or intrusive thoughts and how can we change them?*

What are automatic thoughts?

Automatic thoughts are something that are triggered by a particular event or feeling, that stirs up a negative action, thought or behavior. It causes a reaction in one way or another and this can lead to feelings of anxiety, anger or depression. The word automatic has strong meaning here because if something is automatic, it is robotic, and it happens without thinking as it is an instant reaction. If you think of a machine doing something over and over again, that's how our brain works.

What are intrusive thoughts?

Intrusive thoughts are similar to automatic thoughts, but this is when you get distressed or disturbed by unwanted thoughts or images. Because of these thoughts, you are often triggered to act in a particular way, and you do compulsive things to help you cope with those thoughts. Intrusive thoughts are often intense, but they too happen automatically. Automatic thoughts are often negative thoughts that become a habit, but with intrusive thoughts, we don't want them to occur because of the way they make us feel and act.

Automatic Thought Patterns

Automatic thought patterns are commonly known in the CBT world as Cognitive Distortions. Grohl (2016) suggests that there are 15, but in this book, we have formed ten based on his studies (Ackerman, 2019).[16]

1. Filtering
2. Polarized thinking
3. Overgeneralization
4. Jumping to conclusions
5. Magnification or Minimization
6. Personalization
7. Blaming others
8. Dwell on what we should have done
9. False beliefs
10. Assuming we are always right

Cognitive distortions are categories that help us make sense of our automatic thoughts. The above distortions contribute to the assumptions, problems and beliefs we have in life. We discuss these cognitive distortions in detail in chapter 4. Be sure to check that out.

Cognitive distortions are a habit because our mind gets used to reacting in these negative patterns. Because they are automatic it can be tricky to see how we should react, because we react first and think later. Cognitive Behavioral Therapy is great at helping you to recognize these patterns and challenge or change them. As human beings we learn things all the time, so programming our mind to think or react differently is possible. We just have to learn it and limit ourselves in the same way we limit ourselves to treats when we are on a diet.

Our Rules and Assumptions

There are rules and assumptions we live by that can hold us back and this is exactly why CBT methods are useful because they challenge everything we live by, everything we believe in.

The way you think is something that is programmed into us. For example, sometimes people believe that if they come from a family that has struggled with their finances, they assume that they will always struggle too. In hindsight, it is scary to think that we do not believe that we can do better. Just because we've never had something, doesn't mean we never will.

It's also worth remembering that just because we have always had something, it doesn't mean we can't lose it. Being too complacent can also be a negative way of thinking, because we have to be rational. In contrast to the previous example, someone with money might believe that they can never lose it and that's not always the case. In order to be financially stable, we need to be smart with our money and have strategies or back-up plans in place. Changing all the rules and assumptions you live by that are negative or cause you anguish is at the heart of CBT and it can mean a happier and healthier you!

This chapter has covered the basics around Cognitive Behavioral Therapy, as well as different key techniques to consider, if you want to utilize this type of therapy and make changes in your life. In the next chapter. Now that we know the basics, it's important to learn about the different applications for CBT so that you can start to make a difference in your own life.

Chapter 3 - Applications for CBT

Have you ever felt down? Not quite good enough? Or so anxious that your functionality as a human being is affected? You're not on your own, most people have felt like this.

CBT can be used as a form of therapy for many different things, so we're going to focus on different ways to apply CBT techniques, based on your diagnosis. If you have medical diagnosis already, then you could have a head start. With CBT, treatments focus around both the person and the problem, so this is a great chapter to help you understand the techniques further.

Anxiety and Panic Attacks

You should have heard the word anxious or anxiety on quite a few occasions throughout this book already because CBT is a common treatment for anxiety.

But what exactly is anxiety?

> *Anxiety is that feeling of apprehension and dread that comes with the physical perception that something*

> *bad might happen. It is accompanied by physical symptoms, such as increases in our heartbeat, breathing rate and muscle tension; tightness in the chest and sweating. (Edelman, 2006)*[17]

Anxiety is worry, but it's taken to a whole new level. It happens because we feel that something is about to happen, something that we don't like or want. We all feel anxious now and then, but this is often short-lived. Feeling anxious now and then is perfectly normal. It's that feeling you might get when you're going for that job interview and your heart races before you're called in. After a while, the feeling passes, and you continue with your day as normal.

Anxiety issues are disorders that are much more complex as they disturb our lives. The difference between the two is that anxiety issues or disorders mean that you might be so nervous and anxious that you never actually make the interview. They prevent you from even going. In fact, you may not have even applied for the job in the first place because the very thought of it is so overwhelming. CBT can really help with this.

We feel anxious when we feel that something threatens us. In the case of the job interview, we are threatened by our pride and ego, as we don't want to fail. Afterall, we are competing for a job that we may never get. Threats could be physical, mental, material, psychological, safety or even threats to our confidence and self-esteem. In turn, this influences the way we think and behave.

Severe anxiousness and worry can lead to panic attacks; when we are so worried and anxious that our mind and body start to react in various different ways that we can't control. Some people get chest pains, or their heart races, they can't hear or function properly, and they can even have blank moments and don't know how they got from one place to another. The panic hits an irrational level height that they can't escape from and it can be an awful, and sometimes terrifying experience. This is because we may not know what's going on around us and we become so frightened as we can't control our mind or bodily reactions.

Cognitive Behavioral Therapy is a useful form of therapy for anxiety and panic attacks because:
1. It helps you to explore and rationalize previous events that have created a sense of fear and make sense of them.
2. It helps you identify valuable coping techniques that work for you.
3. It encourages you to think differently and assess the worst-case scenario in a rational way, and the

probability of that actually happening.
4. It gives you focus and challenges you to achieve your progress goals.
5. It prepares and helps you face the situations that stir-up feelings of anxiousness.
6. Because its goal orientated, it keeps you motivated because you can monitor your progress.

Anxiety and panic attacks are something that need to be worked on over a long period of time, but CBT can really help to maintain focus and monitor progression. It can help you get to the bottom of your problems so that you understand the causes and triggers. This means you will have the tools you need to manage and cope with your anxiety and get on with your life before the panic sets in. Plus, if panic does start to creep up on you, you are able to recognize and cope with it before it gets out of control.

Phobias, Post Traumatic Stress Disorder (PTSD), and Obsessive-Compulsive Disorder (OCD)

Phobias, PTSD and OCD are all types of anxiety disorders. An important part of recovery when it comes to these types of anxiety issues is to accept them. These disorders are trickier to manage because they cause a physical reaction that can't be controlled.

Phobias - Anxiety is so intense when you have a phobia because you are consumed by fear. They are irrational and it often means that we blow situations out of proportion because we see them differently.

PTSD - A traumatic event is often the cause of PTSD and they can either be part of this event or simply witness it. The event stays with them, and they often suffer flashbacks of situations they have tried to block out or ignore. It's a high-state of anxiety that sets in feelings of fear and panic. Sometimes sufferers relive the traumatic event.

OCD - Anxiety is significantly elevated with this disorder because a person is often so consumed with rituals and struggle with change. This often stems from a fear that something bad is going to happen and the belief that the rituals will prevent it. People who suffer with OCD often have intrusive thoughts that haunt their mind. They feel a compulsion to prevent it and try to keep busy.

Cognitive Behavioral Therapy helps you to discover the cause of your anxiety disorders and face your fears. This can be traumatic for some people, so it's always important to get a formal diagnosis from a medical professional. CBT is known to be effective, but if the anxiety issues are severe, it's important to seek appropriate help and advice from a medical professional.

Depression

According to Markus MacGill (2017) in Medical News Today, *"Sadness, feeling down, having a loss of interest or pleasure in daily activities"* that persist and are left untreated can develop into depression. They explain that they can begin to hugely affect our life in a substantial way.[18] This definition is accurate because depression is such a broad condition that affects everyone in different ways. There are many scientific studies that express their support for CBT as a successful treatment for depression. This can often be successful with or without medication but remember, if you have been prescribed medication by a medical professional, you should never stop taking this, without professional medical advice.

When a person suffers from depression, they don't see the point of any change because of how they feel. They seem to adopt the negative attitude that nothing is ever going to change for them, and they struggle to see anything positive. People can suffer further symptoms that impact their energy levels; for example, they may lose their appetite or struggle to sleep and concentrate. All of these add to the misery-cloud that depression forms.

Typically, a negative event or experience causes depression, but negative core beliefs and assumptions can certainly build and result in this feeling too. Every person who suffers from depression will likely suffer from different triggers because the condition is individual, but the thoughts, feelings, and actions of a person who suffers from depression can be very similar.

CBT is an effective treatment for depression because:
1. It explores the root cause of your depression, which allows you to face your problems head-on, and focus on solving them.
2. It encourages you to stay focused by aiming for progression goals.
3. It allows you to monitor your progress by encouraging you to record your activities, feelings, thoughts and actions throughout the week.
4. It gives you structure so that you know what to do and when to do it. This can help you if you're strugging to eat and sleep.
5. It can help you to aim for a positive future and know/feel that this is possible.

People who suffer from depression can feel lost and empty. They become almost robotic and this can be a serious condition. Feelings of depression should not be ignored or underestimated, so you should seek advice from a medical professional. A CBT therapist may also be able to help you get to the bottom of your depression.

Anger Management

Anger is an emotion that affects our behavior. It can sometimes explode out and cause us to become extremely irrational. Sometimes a person may suffer with uncontrollable anger if they feel they've been treated unfairly and if they feel threatened, the anger can be intensified. In some cases, anger can be a good thing, because it keeps us motivated and it gives us a sense of power, but we have to be careful because we don't want it to go too far.

Anger can result in us spiraling out of control. Sometimes anger comes from stress and this can sometimes mean we direct it to the wrong place or at the wrong people. Anger can be at different levels and sometimes we let out too much or too little. Holding anger in can be just as explosive as letting it out, because it builds up inside.

CBT can help with anger management because it can help us to take a calm approach and control this effectively. Being mindful can also help to manage and control anger, so it's definitely worth checking out chapter 10 of this book too.

CBT can be helpful when dealing with anger because:
1. It can help the sufferer determine what's causing the anger.
2. If we know what's causing the anger, we can start to

put an appropriate plan of action in place to deal with that.

3. It can help to uncover a range of techniques to help cope with any anger issues or stressful situations effectively.
4. It is goal-orientated, so it provides a focus for the sufferer to concentrate on.
5. CBT is an effective therapy for thoughts, emotions and behavior, and as anger triggers all three, it is an effective method of maintaining control while working through problems.

Anger is a common issue that can be treated quickly and effectively if noticed early on. If it's left alone, it can result in numerous issues including violent outbursts, further mental health issues, and you can even find yourself in trouble legally. This can even spread into depression as you no longer recognize yourself and dislike the person you've become. It can be a long road to recovery, but learning to talk out your worries, as well as being mindful of the situation helps.

Is CBT an Effective Treatment for Children and Adolescents?

Absolutely! CBT is not just for adults; it can be great for both children and adolescents too. There are many reasons for this, but one key reason is because it's flexible and can be offered in many different formats to suit the young person. Therapy can be on a one-to-one basis, in a group, or with parents.

CBT is a useful approach for children and adolescents because it reviews many different coping mechanisms. It provides them with the tools and coping techniques they need to manage several different situations in their life, including stress and anxiety. Young people will work towards targets, so they have clear steps to take and know exactly what to do and because they are young, it is easier for them to adopt the strategies so that they use them naturally.

Young people are often receptive to CBT because the therapist does not tell them what to do but allows them to lead and work out solutions to their problems. This can be invaluable in the future when they are subjected to stressful situations and can generally help the way they think and approach things in their life.

If a young person is suffering from anxiety, depression, anger issues, or negative/emotional behavior, then CBT can be recommended by a medical professional. It has even been recommended in cases of substance misuse or post-traumatic stress disorder.

CBT for children is usually a short-term treatment program delivered by a therapist who uses the sessions to teach CBT skills and techniques to the children and sometimes their parents. In most cases, children, their parents, the therapist, and anyone else involved in the child's life could be involved in the implementation and support with CBT.

There are many different approaches that can be used with children, so it's even more important to work with the right therapist, preferably one who has worked with children in the past. Collaboration is so important, and CBT can actually work as a type of family therapy too (Effective Child Therapy, 2019). [19]

CBT is not restricted by age and has many benefits for all. The key component of CBT is goal setting and problem-solving techniques, but first, you need to identify your problems and your core beliefs, so you can start to move forward.

Chapter 4 – What's my Problem?

You already know that you need to make a change as there's some problem in your life, preventing you from moving forward or being happy. For the next part of the CBT process, we need to work out what your problems are exactly.

Working out what our problems are isn't always easy. When we've thought a certain way or believed a certain thing for a long time, it can be difficult to see that it's causing a problem because it feels natural and normal to us. Often, we know something is wrong, but we don't pinpoint the root cause and we only touch the surface. This means that the problem recurs because the problem isn't solved.

There are a range of strategies we can use to identify problems and then we can use CBT to work on solving those problems. It's time to get to work!

Strategy 1 – Identifying your irrational and negative thinking patterns and actions with Journaling.

Identifying your problems takes time so it's important to be patient at this stage It could take a number of weeks to identify your problems. One simple way of doing this is to use Journaling. Journaling is an important CBT technique if you need to work out what the problem is. It can help you to evaluate the extremity of your problems and how deep they run.

So, what is journaling?

Journaling is a commitment. It's a record of your thoughts, actions and feelings. It's a great way to work through your emotions, actions and thoughts. At first it is a simple record, but as you start to move on in the CBT process, it will prove to be a useful tool to reflect on how you feel, and it often helps you to pinpoint the root cause of your problems. You can describe how you feel, what caused it and how you coped with the situation[20] (Ackerman, 2019) and then when you have enough information, you can analyze this and use a range of further tools to help you take action against those.

Activity 1 – Setting up and Using a Journal

To journal, you need a notebook, or online document to record events from your days. You should set your diary up in a particular way:

At the very top of your journal page for each day, I want you to note down something you are thankful for today, so ensure you leave a prompt at the top of your diary – *Today, I'm thankful for…*

You then need to set up a table of four columns:
Event – So you can note down information about the event that triggered your reaction.
Feelings – How did this make you feel?
Actions – What did you do or how did you act in response to this event?
Thoughts – What thoughts did the event trigger?

You can note down positive and negative events in the table, but you should color-code these (black for negative and green for positive, for instance).

You should also leave a blank space at the end of your page too, so you can make a personal reflection in your journal.

*You need to use your journal every day for a number of weeks. You can assess your thoughts after one week and start to work on further CBT techniques, but you should keep on with your journaling and make it part of your daily routine.

Journaling should be continuous, but you can start to work through and assess your diary after the first 7 days. Once you have enough information, you can start with the next part of your CBT process, and identify your cognitive distortions.

What are Cognitive Distortions?

Cognitive distortions are a collective name for your irrational thoughts and negative thinking patterns. As we explore them, try to relate some of the problems you have identified as part of your journaling process to the different categories. You may also find that other issues crop up, that you haven't really identified as being an issue previously until you've read the definitions and relate how you think, feel and act to these distortions.

Cognitive distortions are key when we start to make sense of our problems as they help us to make sense of our thoughts, feelings and actions. This works hand in hand with journaling and we can identify the negatives problems and then we can start to categorize them. Once we categorize them, we can plan a course of action.

Defining Cognitive Distortions

We've already established that Cognitive Distortions are different types of automatic thoughts. When we have thought in a particular way for so long, we believe it and we continue to think in that way. That's why people who suffer from anxiety and depression have a relapse, because those thoughts and feelings don't just go away. Even if we've worked through our previous issues, we can still have doubt in the back of our mind that creeps through now and then to stir things up. That's why learning to cope is so important. It breaks the cycle, so we are less likely to fall back into old habits and patterns.

Have a read through the descriptions and examples of each below. Grohl (2016) suggests that there are 15, but in this book, we have formed ten based on his studies (Ackerman, 2019)[21]. We will use the ten we've formed below throughout this book:

1. **Filtering** - The way we filter information is complex and often we filter out anything positive and concentrate on the negative.
2. **Polarized thinking** - This is when we are defeated easily because we believe there only two options in life; we either succeed or we fail. If we don't succeed, we just believe we are failure and there is no room to grow or middle ground. Sometimes we simply don't get the desired effect because we need to work on one area, but polarized thinking again focuses on the negative aspects and accepts failure far too easily. This line of thinking

acknowledges only perfection as success, but in reality, perfection is often rare.

3. **Overgeneralization** - This is a cognitive distortion identified by Beck (1967) and this basically means that we allow one single experience to define us. This is like heading to the kitchen and a recipe not going to plan. From that point on, you generalize yourself as being a bad cook. As human beings, we learn from our mistakes and should never put ourselves in a box that prevents growth and development. Cooking is a skill and if we make a mistake, we can learn to cook better next time. That's the case with most things in life. Overgeneralization blocks us from experiencing that learning curve. This can escalate to a more extreme level and affect the way we think about or treat others. It can cause us to judge and mislabel based on generalized assumptions.

4. **Jumping to Conclusions** - This is another way that we block, and it is similar to overgeneralization, except we make judgement calls and assumptions based on nothing. This is like assuming people do not like you or judging you do not like someone without really getting to know them, or that we don't like something without trying it first.

5. **Magnification or Minimization** - This is another distortion that was identified by Beck (1967) and this is when we magnify or catastrophize an event and make it more dramatic than it actually this. This is the mother of blowing something out of proportion. When you magnify an event to this level it is difficult to see clearly because panic sets in. *Does that tiny spelling mistake in an email really mean your reputation is ruined and that your boss will sack you for instance?* Although this isn't professional, others do accept that it is human nature to make occasional mistakes. It is often how we react in response to the mistake that matters. Now, Beck (1967) looks at magnification and minimization as separate entities, but Grohl (2016) counts these two distortions together, because minimization can be just as damaging. Sometimes we minimize the positive things that happen in our life because we focus on the negative. These two distortions often work hand in hand, because we magnify the negative and minimize the positive.

6. **Personalization** -This is another distortion identified by Beck (1967) and this is when we believe we are responsible for certain things that happen. We take things personally and think that something happened because of us or someone

doesn't like us because of something we have done. Often this is us thinking irrationally.

7. **Blaming others** - We can sometimes blame others for how we feel. For example, we can say that we are in a bad mood because of the actions of someone else. In reality, only we are responsible for how we feel.

8. **Dwell on what we should have done** - Often, we have certain expectations of ourselves and we dwell on certain situations in which we don't adhere to those. We reflect on what we should have done, rather than what we did do. We can be hard on ourselves and beat ourselves up over how we should have acted.

9. **False beliefs** - Grohl (2016) talks about different fallacies that we have and how sometimes they are beyond our control, because we believe them to be true. We just accept that things are out of our control, life is unfair, or we have no luck, when something negative happens, without attempting to take back control or trying to rectify the situation. For example, if something bad happens and we think that we are fated to have bad luck and just accept that there is nothing we can do, we have already accepted defeat and we don't even try to win.[22]

10. **Assuming we are always right** - This is another attitude that can hold us back as we can miss opportunities due to being so closed-minded. We have to be willing to try new things but we also shouldn't be afraid to try again, even if something didn't work on the first attempt. Imagine you applied for a job last year, and you didn't get it. You now see the job advertised again and you really want it, but you convince yourself you won't get it because you didn't get it last time. This assumption holds us back because we've already accepted defeat. We've convinced ourselves were not going to get it, so we might apply but not really put the effort in or we might not apply at all. This is because we assume we are right – we'll never get the job.

Do any of these distortions sound familiar? With CBT, we need to take a step back, to identify and assess our cognitive distortions in a logical way. Now you know what distortions are, you can start to categorize your problems with strategy #2.

Strategy 2 – Identifying and Making Sense of Cognitive Distortions

The first step to resolving cognitive distortions is to identify what is causing us these roadblocks. This can be done with or without a therapist, although if you are having trouble identifying and categorizing your problems at first, a therapist can help you to do this.

You should now have your journal and you will have filled this with at least 7 days of content, so you have an idea of the kinds of problems you face.

You should now focus on the events that initiated a negative feeling, thought or reaction, and attach them to one of the ten cognitive distortions that we've discussed earlier in this chapter. You then need to analyze these distortions in a logical way.

What evidence suggests this? What are my distortions based on? You might surprise yourself here because you may have more negative thought patterns than you think. You really need to put on your objectivity hat at this point and you can start to unravel those thoughts and begin to set goals to change these beliefs. Once you identify the problematic areas and approach them in an objective and logical way, the easier it becomes to challenge them and change them. Don't hold back!

Activity 2 – Making Sense of it all

Take your journal, and highlight all of the negative thoughts, feelings and actions that you've identified.

Make a table (you can draw this or create a digital/printable document) that includes the following columns:

Event	Feeling/Thought/Action	Cognitive Distortion	My ideal
Ran into someone at a party who used to bully me at school.	Felt angry, upset. Caused me to be snappy with others and leave the party early.	Blaming others.	Not to feel like I've done something wrong and should leave. I want to feel comfortable enough to stay and move on.

You need to note down the events from your journal in your table. You have to note down what you felt, thought and how you acted as a resulted. You then need to categorize the distortion. Above we use blaming others as our cognitive distortion in the example, now this doesn't mean that the bully is blameless. Bullying is terrible, but for this exercise, if we think it's someone else's fault for the way we act/feel/think then we are blaming others. Maybe it is their fault and that's fine, but this process isn't about them, it's about you right now and how you can make a change. In the ideal part, simply make a comment on your ideal situation. *How did you want to act/feel/think?*

Once you've got them all down on paper and categorized, the fun can begin.

To start unravelling your cognitive distortions, you need to focus on the distortions that you personally suffer from and think about how these harmful automatic thoughts hold you back. Look again at the example in the activity above. That person would lose out on being at the party and lose out on having fun, all because of events from the past and one person. Once we start to recognize our cognitive distortions, we start to understand why we feel or act in a particular way. We can also dig a little deeper to gain a more in depth understanding. Using the questions in activity 3 can help you get to grips with your cognitive distortions and really begin to understand them.

Activity 3 – Why?

Look closely at your cognitive distortions and make some notes on the following questions as they will help you figure out why you feel the way you do;
- What triggered the reaction exactly (something/one you seen, heard, a song perhaps)?
- Why do you think you think you reacted in that way?
- What's the worst that could happen if you faced this?
- What would make the situation easier for you, or ease your worries?

The whole strategy of identifying and making sense of your thoughts, actions and feelings is generally an effective method of therapy because you can do this in your own time and at your own pace. Once you change your frame of mind, become aware and use logic to assess your distortions, you are left with the ability to do this regularly and it will become a natural process. This is an easy maintenance strategy as you can continue to do this for as long as your journal, but hopefully your negative events will become less and less.

Cognitive distortions are a habit because our mind gets used to reacting in these negative patterns. Because they are automatic it can be tricky to see how we *should* react, because we react first and think later. CBT techniques are great at helping you to recognize those patterns and feeling able to challenge or change them. As human beings we learn things all the time, so programming our mind to think or react differently is possible. We just have to learn the skills.

Chapter 5 – Going Deeper into your Problems

You've identified your problems and that's a big step, so you should give yourself a pat on the back. Chapter 4 was a heavy chapter that focused on finding your present problems which is great. CBT focuses on the now, but you have to remember that every problem has a cause and sometimes that cause is deeper than you think.

In this chapter, we're going to focus on identifying and assessing problems that link to the way our body reacts, and we'll also consider how problems link to the beliefs we have. It's important to know the nitty-gritty before you devise a plan of action to overcome these. It's about raising awareness for now, so that you can bridge the gap between your problems and how they can have a deeper meaning.

Strategy 3 – Identifying, Assessing and Challenging Bodily Reactions

We have bodily reactions when we are sick, stressed or depressed. We've also talked about the bodily reactions we face when we suffer from a panic attack. Think about how your state of mind is affected by your negative behaviors or thoughts… Well it can also affect our body and cause a reaction. Sometimes when we assess our problems, we don't consider the impact it has on us wholly.

Sometimes events that trigger feelings, thoughts and reactions can affect our appetite and sleeping patterns, we can feel or actually be physically sick from the pit of our stomach, or we can even bring on our very own stress headache. *But why?*

Well, the body is a funny thing and like our mind, we sometimes have very little control over how it responds to certain situations. It's time to assess how our body is affected by the way we feel so that we can change. CBT is not only about changing the thoughts and the way we feel, it's about changing behavior too and the impact that all these things have on us. It's an all-rounded approach, that focuses on tackling all issues and encourages you to make choices that are better for your state of mind and health.

Activity 4 – How to Identify your Bodily Reactions

1. Reflect back on your journal, and your work from activity 2.
2. Pick 2 or 3 key events that had the most distressing impact on you.
3. Note them down in a notebook, in the back of your journal or a separate piece of paper and approach each event in turn.
4. Think about this event and focus on how it made you feel, what it made you think and how you reacted. Now, think about how your body reacted and write this down. Did you keep thinking or reliving this event in your head? How long did the reaction last for (minutes, several days...)? Note down your responses.
5. Repeat step 4 for each key event you've noted down.

Sometimes our reactions last for 5-minutes, while others play on our minds and affect us for a number of days or weeks, so it's important to pinpoint this. Maybe it's still bothering you right now.

This strategy can be used alongside both your journaling and when you're resolving your cognitive distortions. Again, it's about recognizing how your body is affected in the first instance, and then afterwards, it's about assessing and challenging those reactions, so you can think about how you can remedy them.

Don't underestimate the power of identifying, assessing and challenging your bodily reactions because it can be a powerful journey that can hit you in an emotional way. If you're ready, it's time to take your first step.

You've identified your bodily reactions to different situations and that's certainly the first step. Awareness is important because if you want so to stop feeling, thinking and reacting differently, you need to recognize what is wrong to enable you to make a change.

Now, it's time to assess and challenge those reaction, based on what you now know. The good thing about this strategy, is that it's personal to you. Sometimes people who feel stress, anxiety and depression can make themselves ill without realizing it, so assessing and challenging your reactions isn't always easy.

Activity 5- Assessing and Challenging your Bodily Reactions

Throughout the course of this activity, you will need to reflect on what you know from activity 4.

Analyze
Look for patterns and correlations between the way you think, feel and act, to the way your body has reacted. For example, if you were put in a stressful situation more than once, take yourself back to that day of the event and the days that follow and ask yourself the awkward questions:

How did my body react?
How does that correlate with the next event?
How was my appetite?
How did I sleep?
How was my mood/stress-levels?
Was I depressed/anxious?
Did I feel unwell/tired/unsocial on that day and the days that follow?
Is this normal for me?
How was I the day before this event?
When was I next/last happy?

Make some statements about your reactions to summarize your bodily reactions.

For example, every time I become anxious, I don't sleep and become unsocial, so I shut myself off from the world to regroup my thoughts. OR, every time I'm stressed out, I become moody and lose my appetite for 3 days.

> ***Challenge***
> You have started to recognize that your body reacts in a particular way to certain events. You can use this to your advantage by challenging and targeting your reactions.
>
> If we use one of the examples from above:
> *Every time I become anxious, I don't sleep, and I become unsocial, so I shut myself off from the world to regroup my thoughts.* There are four problems – the anxiousness, the lack of sleep, being unsocial, cutting ourselves off from the world. Why (and other problem questions) is always a good place to start. *Ask yourself why we feel or react in this way? What is it that we fear?*

By asking probing questions, we're challenging our reactions and although this may not remedy the immediate issues, being aware helps because we begin to understand why we react, feel and think in a particular way.

The purpose of activity 5 was not change those bodily reactions (at least not just yet) but to analyze and challenge them. Awareness is everything and it allows us to understand our own thoughts, emotions and behaviors, which is the first step in remedying issues.

In relation to activity 5, if we did not become anxious in the first place, we would not trigger the bodily reactions such as sleep issues, and the need to be unsocial. That means we can target the problem at its core.

Chapter 3 has already talked through anxiety and anxiety disorders, phobias, PTSD, OCD, Depression and Anger. Each of those conditions can trigger bodily reactions but they can also be targeted using CBT strategies. If you feel stressed, your mood dips, or you don't sleep well, strategies such as relaxed breathing, muscle relaxation are discussed in chapter 7 and they will be great for you. Other techniques such as assertiveness and awareness training are covered in chapter 9, and you should also check out Mindfulness Based Cognitive Therapy in chapter 10. All of the strategies covered in this book, will help you to address the bodily reactions that you've recognized here.

Strategy 4 - Assessing Problem Causes Using the ABC Model

The ABC model is instrumental in CBT because it was one of the very first strategies to be introduced. You may have heard this mentioned earlier, in chapter 1 as this model was created by Ellis (1957 but it's certainly an effective model to use if you want to identify begin to understand and change your own behavior. In this section, we are looking at the ABC model to raise awareness of the beliefs we might have that influence our negative thoughts. In chapter 6, we will push this further and challenge our whole belief system.

The ABC Model is based on behavioral therapy, and again,

you can use a worksheet or table to record your problematic areas and to recognize the impact they have. We are programmed to react in a negative or irrational way, and the idea behind the ABC model, is to challenge our beliefs and the way we think.

To use the *ABC* model effectively, you need to use the first column to highlight your Activating event or objective situation. This means that you note down an event that happens that leads to a highly emotional response or causes you to think negatively. In the second column you need to write down the details of your response down - say what happened and how you feel. This will represent your beliefs and what you believe about yourself or your problem. In the final column you should discuss the impact. Here, you should bridge the differences between the initial event and the distress it causes you:

Look at the table below to see an example of how a single event can cause an irrational belief and this can mean result in negative consequences. It is important for us to make a change and turn that negative or irrational belief, into something rational. Then we can start to behave in a positive way. If we behave in a positive way to a bad situation, the more likely we are to succeed in the future.

	Irrational	*Rational*
A - Activating Event	Failed driving test	Failed driving test
B - Belief	Must pass the driving test on the first attempt.	<u>Would like</u> to have passed the driving test on the first attempt.
C - Consequence	Negative feelings of sadness, depression, anger, worthlessness.	Healthy feelings of sadness, and disappointment. Feeling of determination to pass next time.

It is important to remember that we have healthy core beliefs as well as the irrational ones and sometimes irrational thoughts comes naturally to us. They fuel our recurring automatic and intrusive thought patterns and this an impact on our state of mind. It is common to assume that we have to pass our driving test, or any test for that matter, on our first attempt. Although this would be encouraged, there is nothing to say that we should give up or cannot try again as sometimes we accept defeat and assume failure. This is a false belief. As human beings, we tend to fill our heads with false beliefs that only end up holding us back in the longer term.

If we are consumed by feelings of sadness, depression, anger and worthlessness, we will never feel good enough to pass the test and this will lead to anxiety, depression and stress because those negative feelings consume us. If we accept that we did not pass, we can start to move forward. Sure, we will be sad and disappointed initially, but we can use those feelings to fuel determination. Determination motivates us and encourages us to work harder and smarter. In the activity below, we will use the ABC model to assess our thought patterns and raise awareness of how our personal beliefs can trigger irrational thoughts and hold us back.

Activity 6

For your next activity, you should make your own version of the table above and use some of the events from your journal and assess them, based on the ABC Model. 2-3 events will be sufficient to begin with, because for now, we're simply raising awareness of our beliefs rather than changing them.

Detail the activating event and then your beliefs on a rational and irrational level. Be honest with yourself when it comes to your irrational feeling. You will already be aware that this is irrational, but you can only challenge this in the future if this you are honest.

You then need to detail the consequences. *What are the consequences of your irrational thought? What are the consequences of your rational thoughts?*

*Repeat this sequence for some of the other events in your journal and then examine your responses in the table. *Can you see how our beliefs hold us back and stop us from moving forward?*

Now that you have started to dig deeper into your thoughts, you will begin to understand how our thoughts, feelings and actions are triggered and how there can be a much deeper root cause that stems from our core beliefs. This helps you to define your problems

Defining Problems

Defining your problems is a key process when you dig deeper and by following the ABC Model, you have already started to do this. CBT is a lifestyle change and although it focuses on the now, it's still important to look at the root causes of your problems.

You should continue with the ABC Model and working on your journal throughout your CBT journey. Don't forget to review your main issues and assess your problems as this will allow you to target them by setting goals, which we will focus on in chapter 7.

The ABC model outlines two types of negative thinking patterns; rational thought which are healthy and irrational thoughts that are unhealthy. We are not robots, so it is healthy for us to feel emotional, to react irrationally and to think negatively from time-to-time but you need to ensure you are aware of these patterns and reacting in a reasonable way. Defining our problems and challenging their root cause prevents us from amplifying issues. It's important that you can differentiate between the two, in order to define your goals effectively.

Once you have defined your problems using your journal and the ABC model, you are ready to really start challenging your core beliefs.

Remember, you are making a transformation here, so be patient. It's really important that you use probing questions to assess your own behavior, thoughts and feelings. To investigate your problems further, you can ask yourself the following questions.

- How did I feel or act (think about your symptoms and the intensity level)?
- What happened to make me feel or react like that (trigger)?
- When did I feel like this and has this happened before (look for patterns)?
- Why did I feel or react like that?

You can note down your answers and keep them with your journal and the other activities you've completed while reading this book.

We will work on changing our core beliefs in chapter 6, so keep this table and apply relevant events to this model and assess them. For now just be conscious of how your beliefs can have an emotional impact by triggering an irrational thought.

Chapter 6 - Identify and Challenge your Core Beliefs

How hard is it to change your whole belief system? Well, when you've believed something your whole life or at least for a long time, it's certainly not easy to make that change. This is why we would suggest that CBT is a lifestyle change as it's so much more than simply resolving problems. Although CBT concentrates on the now, it's still important to go back and challenge your core beliefs. You've already started to do that in chapter 5 of this book, with the ABC Model and now it's time to challenge your whole belief system. *Are you ready?*

Mistakes

Sometimes we make mistakes in our lives and we can be really hard on ourselves. It can take us a long time to forgive ourselves and this can have a major impact on us. It's human nature to make mistakes but we have to have a certain level of acceptance too. We have to accept ourselves.

How long do you punish yourself if you make a mistake?

You see, it's not the actual act of making a mistake that holds us back, it's the way we cope with it. If we don't cope well and can't accept that mistakes are human nature, it can put us off taking risks in future as we won't feel this way again. The way we think, react and feel as a result of a mistake can create a fear of failure. This fear then holds us back as we stop seeing the worth in taking risks because we are so afraid of making mistakes and this can keep us from success in the future.

The sooner we accept that we make mistakes, and change our mindset surrounding them the sooner we can move on. Mistakes can actually be a good thing from the perspective that if we are making mistakes, we are learning something.
If we treat mistakes as a learning curve, it can have a positive impact on our life. It is rare that we make the same mistake twice and next time we take a risk, we might reflect on a previous mistake which means the next time we take a risk, the more chance we have of being successful.

Success isn't meant to be easy. If it was so easy, then we wouldn't view it in such high standing. Giving up is the easy way out and by holding back because we fear the consequences of our mistakes makes us stagnant. If you accept your mistakes, learn from them, then you are leaving room for personal growth. If you do things right next time, imagine how accomplished you will feel.
What have you learned from your mistakes?

This leads us to our next strategy.

Strategy 5 - Self-Acceptance

You need to accept yourself and accept that we all make mistakes. It is natural to want to do better than we already do, but we can't be the best in all areas. We have to have a certain form of acceptance. We can make improvements and we can play on our own strengths. Sometimes we wish we could do something else or be someone else, but it has to be within our remit and capabilities. Disappointment is normal!

Activity 7 – Self-acceptance exercise – Taking your own Advice

Look at your journal and reflect on one mistake you've made, or something about yourself that you don't like. This should be a something that really stands out for you and has instilled some fear. *You never want to experience that feeling, thought or action again!*

Imagine that a friend or family member feels like this or has made this mistake and they're distraught. What advice would you give them?

The purpose of activity 7 is to recognize what advice you would give another person, so you can see how harsh you are being on yourself. We often think or feel things about ourselves, or act in a specific way but we beat ourselves up and blow it out of proportion. In hindsight, you won't be the first person who had that thought or made that type of mistake and you certainly won't be the last.

How would you feel if you found out that at least 5 other people you know have felt or acted that way or made a similar mistake? Imagine that this includes the most confident person you know and wouldn't expect. *What if you found out, they felt or acted in exactly the same as you did, but they handled it differently?*

In truth, many people (if not all) will have experienced the same things. The only thing they did differently, is own their mistakes or feelings.

Owning up to how we feel or what we did is a tool we can use to do better next time by thinking about what we might do differently. We can then show acceptance and move on. The others who experienced the same feelings as you didn't dwell on what they should or shouldn't have done and allow their feelings to turn into fear. They simply learned and moved on and you can do the same:

1. Go back to your answers from activity 7.
2. Note down what you would do differently.
3. Admit what you did 'I did [this]...' Come on, say it out loud!
4. Ask yourself, what have I learned from this?
5. Fill in the blanks and repeat this mantra, several times if need be: *I did [action/mistake/feeling], but it's okay because I've learned [what have you learned?] and next time, I'll do [what will you do differently].*

When you come to terms with your own mistakes, feelings and actions you can use it to your advantage. Many inspirational people in the world reflect on past experiences to help others. A business owner might speak at an event and tell you everything they did wrong, before they did something right.

The things we experience in life are a learning curve as they help us grow and reflect. It's time to ditch that old negative belief we have when it comes feeling like we've made a mistake or have acted inappropriately. Our experiences can sometimes be painful, but they can also indicate strength and shape us a person.

Keep repeating your own personal mantras for each experience in your journal when you have struggled to accept yourself or a mistake, until you have addressed each of them. You can work and build on these and turn them into something positive.
If we use them in the right way, we can even use them to motivate and inspire!

Core Beliefs

Your core beliefs are at the heart of everything you do. We can't help but to live by these beliefs because we strongly believe in them, either consciously or subconsciously. They stem from our past and they influence the way we view the world, the people in it, and how we live our lives.

Our core beliefs are often instilled inside us, but have you ever thought that they could actually be holding us back? Unraveling your core beliefs can take time, much more time than it can to unravel a problem and it also takes some time to reprogram them too as they usually all link together and they challenge the way you make sense of everything.

Our core beliefs are split into three categories; the beliefs we have in ourselves, the beliefs we have in others, and the beliefs we have in the world/life.

For example, if you think you are not smart enough to progress in your career, you might believe that others will never promote you because they don't respect you, and then you may believe that the world is against you and you'll never be able to make anything of your life.

Core beliefs of this sort are toxic because it is such an untrue and negative outlook on yourself and the world around you. This could prevent you from applying for a promotion in the future, as you will not want to take the risk due to the fear instilled. They are the root cause of anxiety, stress, depression and confidence issues. They instill feelings of worthlessness, because a person can truly believe that there's no room for growth. *But where's the proof?*

These core beliefs are completely unfounded and yet the longer we let them fester, the worse we feel. This is a form of self-torture and yet, there's no reason to do this to ourselves. Some of our core beliefs are less obvious and it can be tricky to start to recognize and unravel them. Beliefs are something we can live by since birth as they can be passed down to us. *So, how can we find out what they are?*

We've already spent time using the ABC Model to identify some of our core beliefs but there are some other techniques we can use if we're struggling to work them out. Sometimes we just have to rephrase and reframe our ideas.

We need to analyze our beliefs in more detail just like how we categorized our problems with cognitive distortions in the earlier chapters. Follow the step-by-step process in the following activity to start recognizing your core beliefs. You can use your journal or the information from the work that you've already completed with the ABC model so that you can sort your beliefs into the three belief categories (beliefs in ourselves, in others, and for the world/life)

Activity 8 – Exploring your Core Beliefs

- Note down the situation that caused your initial problem and focus on how you felt or acted. What was the negative aspect?
- Really think about what this says about you. What do you think it suggests?
- Keep asking yourself why. Why did I feel like that? Why did I act like that?
- What do you think others will think about this?
- Why will they think that? Do you have any proof that people think this or is an assumption?
- What does this mean about the world or life?
- Why do you think the world will think or react like this? Again, what proof do you have of this?
- Look at your beliefs. Are there any common themes? For example, say your beliefs all point to a lack of self-belief, that's your theme. You then need to question why you have this self-belief and form your own probing questions based on your beliefs. When was the last time you really believed in yourself? What happened to make you stop believing in yourself?

These beliefs ultimately shape the way you view the world and while some beliefs we have are fine, others can set us on a downward spiral. We need to target these assumptions and beliefs to enable us to let go of the past and move forward.

Facing Problems, Assumptions and Beliefs Head-on

If you want to face your problems, beliefs and assumptions, you must get to the root cause so that you can begin to target these. As you know, CBT generally involves targeting the present but if your core assumptions and beliefs stem from things that have happened in the past this can take a little experimentation as we aren't always clear.

To face your problems, assumptions and beliefs, we have to think about instrumental things that have happened in the past and think about how they've had a negative impact on what you believe about yourself, others and the world. Sometimes you can pin-point these yourself easily, but to get to the core, sometimes we need to experiment and record different events that provoke a reaction.

We can only target these, once we know what they are. *But how do we find out?* Exposure planning is a great strategy used to identify, challenge and monitor your problems and core beliefs. It targets the assumptions and beliefs directly and can be very effective.

Strategy 6 - Exposure Planning

Exposure Planning is a great technique in CBT that can be used to help us figure out and target our problems and assumptions. It can be effective, but it can also be quite emotional, and usually it's because of the sense of relief and realization you feel. Exposing yourself to certain situations can be an exhilarating experience. It helps you to train your mind to do something in a different way and with this technique, you get to test your own limits. It's a great way of figuring out what works for you.

This technique involves you thinking about your typical day and the type of things you do. You can make a list of the behaviors that you should be avoiding or want to change. This method is great for things like OCD because you expose yourself to the typical situation that you usually react to, but you then respond to the compulsion in a different way. Listing what you usually do shows awareness of what the problematic behaviors are, and the exposure really helps you to start coping with everyday situations differently.

Activity 9 – Plan your Exposure

- Have a look in your journal from the last week, or your ABC Model and choose some regular events that set off your anxiety or cause some discomfort or distress. It must be something that you're willing to confront.
- Look at your notes and really think about how you feel and how you usually respond.
- Think about how you could respond in a rational and better way (how do you want to think, feel, act, next time this happens?).
- What does it suggest about your problems and your core beliefs?
- Make a plan to expose yourself to a situation or event that will spark this feeling.

Triggering event	Exposure activity	Day/time of 1st exposure	Day/time of 2nd exposure	Outcome after 2nd exposure
What event triggered the feelings, thoughts and actions?	What happened last time? What will you do to avoid or cope with the situation? How?	Date and time of exposure activity.	Date and time of 2nd exposure activity.	How do you feel after the 2nd exposure? Did it get easier? How successful was it? What did you do differently?

Understanding your Assumptions and Beliefs

Once you've considered some events in your life that have had a negative impact, you then need to really think of the decisions or assumptions you make because of those beliefs.

We use our beliefs to set rules in our own lives, and they often impact on the way we react to something. If we refer back to the ABC model, we can start to think about the root cause of these assumptions and unpick our belief system. At the start of this chapter, we started to discuss the three categories of our core beliefs; the beliefs we have about ourselves, about others, about life and the world. *Just take some time to reflect on activity 9 and think about the beliefs you have that make you think, feel or act the way that you do when you encounter an event that triggers a negative reaction/thought.*

For example, if someone in your family had issues with alcohol throughout your childhood and made us miserable, we may associate this idea of alcohol and misery throughout our life. This is a belief we adopt but it's not necessarily true. This is not to suggest that alcohol is good in any way, but someone who has an occasional tipple would not necessarily spread consistent misery.

Our fear that it does, would make us avoid situations or

people involved in alcohol because we link it closely to misery, when in fact, we could find a great friend or colleague in someone that has an occasional drink. They could also be very happy and positive people but our experience and negative association forms how we think and feel about people or an occasion. Maybe we would also avoid establishments that serve alcohol if the fear grows further and this could hold us back as a result as we would miss out on social occasions too. Many people enter places even if they don't drink alcohol, for the social aspect.

Fear is something that can fuel our false beliefs. When something bad happens to us, we make certain assumptions and form certain beliefs. Often, we are prompted by fear, because we don't want to feel, think or act in the way we previously did.

It is time to start working with those negative core beliefs that are holding you back, as this will help you to improve and grow. They can be a weakness of ours and it's really important to address them and flip them around. You've already started to target your beliefs and assumptions by exposure planning, but we need to push further. Rather than feeling bad or reacting to your core beliefs, we should challenge them and think of other ways to deal with this in an open and positive way. This growth journey is much more valuable if you learn something or grow personally as a result. This is something we can be proud of!

Strategy 7 Directly Targeting your Negative Core Beliefs

Negative core beliefs are common but if you keep targeting them and challenging them, you will start to alter the way you feel. Once you have explored your beliefs and assumptions with the ABC Model, you can begin to do this.

Activity 10 – Targeting Negative Belief statements

Sometimes we believe in something and then we change our mind. For a long time, you may use a specific brand of cereal and because you believe in them, you continue to buy them. Maybe your whole family buys them, and you've never tried anything else. But you go to store to buy some, and they don't have any. You go to the next store, but they don't either, so you have to buy another. You've convinced yourself you won't like them. After lots of resistance, you try them and you're pleasantly surprised. The next time you go to the store and pick up your regular brand, you might think twice. Now, you wouldn't necessarily change your brand, but you now know the other brand is okay. It might take some time for you to make the change because habits make us comfortable. We may be more open to change now as a result of this experience - we just need to change our habit, assumption or belief.

In this activity, we're going to challenge our core beliefs, once we work them out. Going back to the driving test example, when we first looked at the ABC Model:
Belief: I must pass my driving test on my first attempt.

Based on this, our core belief is: *Failure is not an option*. There isn't a law that says we can't re-sit the driving test (or retake any test for that matter). This belief is false, it's irrational and it's unfounded. You need to respond to your core beliefs in a motivational way. Take a look at the example below:

Current Core Belief	Response to this belief
Failure is not an option	*I treat not winning or getting the results I want as a learning curve. Whenever I feel like I've failed or could've done better, I don't give up. I get back up, dust myself off, and feel more motivated than ever to do better next time.*

If a family or friend came to you with this belief, you wouldn't say Sure, you're a failure, that's it for you now. So, why do we do this to ourselves?

We are often our own biggest critic, when we should be a fan. We have the power to motivate ourselves and to make the change we crave.

Activity:
1. Make a table like the one above and make a list of your core values, assumptions and beliefs (you can use your journal, ABC model or any of the earlier activities to help you).
2. Get to the heart of your core belief and find out what it really means.
3. Make a positive statement in response to each of these.
4. Display these somewhere you can see them (post it notes on the wall, your notice board, or in the front of diary). You can refer to them whenever you have doubts.

Remember, we formed our belief system in the first place, so we can change it!

Once you target your negative beliefs, you can start to cope with these better and you could even come up with strategies or ways to avoid your triggers. Having statements in response to negative beliefs is a great motivator because it really highlights how irrational we are being. They also give you a basis to start forming your new, positive and rational core beliefs.

Identifying your negative core beliefs can be daunting because we are not just challenging one idea here, we are challenging everything you believe in and sometimes we realize that those things we've lived by are unfounded and they are often responsible for our stress, anxiety, depression, behavior and negativity.

On the flip side, forming your new core beliefs can be refreshing. It can give you a new power or lease of life, and you can start to really change your outlook on life. You can do this right now! Take your table from activity 10 and form new core beliefs. Let's go back to the failing a driving test one more time: *Failure helps me grow.*

You can expand your points if you want, but this is the top and bottom of the belief. Failure helps us grow because we can learn from it, we can feel motivated and it can make us a stronger person.

This chapter is quite heavy, so if you're feeling overwhelmed right now, the strategies in the next chapter will help to calm your mind and help you refocus.

Chapter 7 – Relax, Regroup, and Believe

Are you ready to relax? The last few chapters have been deep, but you survived it and now it's time for some self-care. It's important to care for yourself, and relaxation can calm your mind and body. This is all part of the CBT process, so we're not straying from our pathway. Often, the importance of caring for oneself is not highlighted enough. We're still going to be working on beliefs in this chapter, but we're going to regroup.

To start, we're going to breathe! Of course, you're breathing right now, but we're going to learn some relaxed breathing. At the beginning of the book you were asked to approach CBT with an open mind, so even if you think this kind of thing isn't for you, you should still give it a try.

Strategy 8 – Relaxed breathing techniques

Working on your problems and beliefs can be overwhelming. It can trigger all sorts of anxiety and emotion. Relaxed breathing techniques can be used in CBT and they are particularly useful if we feel like we're on an emotional rollercoaster. They can help us to calm the mind and they can also help us to focus and think in a rational way. If we are working on our core beliefs, it's more important than ever for us to be rational. Relaxed breathing can be especially useful if you have panic attacks or anxiety disorders.

This technique may be similar to mindfulness, but you will simply focus on your breathing. As the whole of chapter 10 is dedicated to mindfulness, we're not going to go too deeply into this right now, we are simply concentrating on using breathing techniques.

Breathing techniques can help us to calm down our mind and body, and this allows us to collect ourselves and then we can reassess our problems. They are great for the present, and they can be built into our routine so that we are more likely to have a stress or anxiety-free day.

If you still aren't sure about your core beliefs or problems, you may be suffering a block. Take some time to relax and reflect, as this could help you focus and figure them out.

Activity 11 – Relax and Reflect

- ✓ Find a relaxed position in either a sitting or laying position. Make sure you don't cross your arms and legs.
- ✓ Ensure you're somewhere quiet. It can be best if you are alone.
- ✓ Close your eyes and listen carefully.
- ✓ Breathe in for 5 seconds through the nose if possible. Hold for 1 second. Then breath out through the mouth for 5 seconds.
- ✓ Repeat the process around 10 times to regulate your breathing – you should be able to hear yourself breathe. Really concentrate.
- ✓ Your arms, legs and head should all feel relaxed and heavy.
- ✓ Fall into a natural breathing rhythm and focus on the breathing and how your chest rises and falls. Do this for a few minutes until you feel calm.
- ✓ When you're ready, open your eyes.
- ✓ Stay in the relaxed position but reflect back on the thing you were doing before the overwhelming feeling kicked in. Give yourself some time to process this idea or thought again.
- ✓ If you start to feel overwhelmed again, return to the breathing technique – in for 5 seconds, hold for 1 second, out for 5 seconds.

There are alternative ways to help you control your breathing too. If you are a visual person, you can imagine images in your mind to focus on, or if you would prefer not to close your eyes, you can focus on an image. You can also play relaxing music in the background and then kick back to practice your breathing. The whole idea of relaxed breathing is to help you relax, so it's important that you find your own rhythm and do what works for you.

We all relax in different ways and when we are relaxed, we can calm ourselves and this means we tend to act in a more rational and effective way. This can certainly help if you suffer with anxiety, panic disorder and OCD because breathing can help you to cope. Being able to calm yourself helps you to maintain control. Breathing can even help with depression too (Ackerman, 2019).[23]

Now, the breathing activity is all well and good, but it doesn't explore the root of your problem or belief. The relaxed breathing technique can help you focus and encourage you to stay calm, but it's important you note this event in your journal and detail its triggers.

If you struggled when you were exploring your core beliefs, relaxed breathing should have helped you clear your mind and focus, so you can now return to that. If you managed to explore your core beliefs and you've already addressed them and written your new, positive beliefs, then you can move on comfortably to the next session, as we're going to move those beliefs from your intellect to your essence.

Move Beliefs from your Intellect to your Essence

If you want to move your beliefs from your intellect to your essence, you need to start reflecting on your new beliefs and consider the event that triggered the emotions, actions and feelings you experienced as a result of these beliefs.

Forming new core beliefs is instrumental if you want to change the way you think, act and feel. You have started to do this already, but as you continue on your CBT journey, more of these will arise, so it's important that you keep recording events in your journal, and assessing your problems, so that you can explore your core beliefs. You should continue to address the negatives by listing positive statements as you did in activity 10.

This will take time as you really need to dig deep. It is possible to make progress with self-help techniques, providing you can be open and honest with yourself and recognize your core beliefs but sometimes people choose a therapist.

You should regularly remind yourself of your new core beliefs and this is most effective if it's in a visual way. It's a great idea to note them down in your journal and remind yourself of them every morning. Alternatively, you could put them on cards and display them on your notice board, or you could create a vision board that details all of your newly formed beliefs.

Whenever you repeat your negative thinking patterns and feel like you are reverting to your old ways of thinking and acting, you need to be able to access and reflect on your new core beliefs. Really reinforce them and push the positive aspects until you believe them without question.

Once you've put your new beliefs into action and you're starting to embed them in your brain, it's time to working on flipping your negativity into creativity.

Negativity versus Creativity

Creativity is the driving force of motivation and positivity. If you typically react, or think in a negative way, creativity could be your savior. Creativity can be a therapeutic outlet within itself and there are many benefits to this. In life, we no longer have room for these negative thought patterns or reactions as our way of thinking changes. This is because we are starting to adopt our new beliefs, so we will now use our negativity for the greater good; to enhance creativity.

Being creative means to be bold, confident, and unafraid to make mistakes or fail. Creative people are driven, and never give up. Maybe you're saying *that's not me!* And right now, it might not be, BUT why can't it be you in the future?

Before you focus on transforming those negative feelings and reactions by using your creativity, we need to clear the mind and alleviate life's stresses. We are going to push relaxed breathing further, by dipping into muscle relaxation. This is a great technique that will certainly help you to clear your mind, focus on creativity and prepare you for the mindfulness work in chapter 10.

Strategy 9 - Muscle relaxation

If you enjoy things like mindfulness already, this is very similar to a mindfulness technique. We will discuss mindfulness in more detail in chapter 10 of this book but for now, we are going to focus on muscle relaxation.

If panic sets in or we are depressed, anxious or stressed, it becomes really difficult for us to think straight. When we are relaxed and can clear our mind from the daily stresses, we can start to think in a more rational and effective way. Whilst breathing relaxation can be great, muscle relaxation takes it just one step further.

Like muscle relaxation techniques, it can calm us because it too involves controlled breathing and then you begin to focus on relaxing your muscles in turn, rather than breathing. You do this until you and your body are in a fully relaxed state. Follow these steps to try muscle relaxation.

Activity 12 – Timed Muscle Relaxation

- ✓ Take yourself off to a quiet place, preferably somewhere you can lie down.
- ✓ Set your alarm for either 10 or 15 minutes.
- ✓ Tell yourself what time the alarm will sound – say it out loud and imagine the sound of your alarm in your head.
- ✓ Lay in a relaxed state. Don't cross any part of your body.
- ✓ Start breathing through your nose, in for 5 seconds, hold for 1 second, and out for 7 seconds.
- ✓ This will send a relaxing feeling through your body, allow it to flow from your shoulders, down, until it reaches your fingertips and then down your body to your toes.
- ✓ Your arms will feel heavy and you should continue to breathe, until you are in a fully relaxed state and then you can start to find your own breathing rhythm.
- ✓ Lay, in your relaxed state until your alarm sounds.
- ✓ You may wish to stay down for few minutes and refocus on your problems or issues, or you may just want to collect your thoughts.
- ✓ Take a couple of deep breaths before you sit up and ensure you move slowly, at your own pace.

This technique can help you to destress, calm your nerves and soothe your mind. A few minutes of this can help you focus on key issues and resolve them in a rational way. If you have not done this before, you can find guidance through online videos on platforms such as Youtube.

Some people prefer to be guided, while others, once they understand what they need to do, prefer to control this themselves, without guidance. You can simply use soothing music if that helps but ultimately, it is important to find the method that suits you the most, individually.

You should take time to enjoy the relaxation techniques. At the end, you still need to be able to rationalize your thoughts so you can use some of the activities at the end of this chapter to help you find solutions or change negative thinking patterns.

You will now be ready to face the world and tap into your creativity.

Turn your Negativity into Creativity

As you start to change your core beliefs, thinking patterns and actions, there's absolutely no reason why you can't be creative. Believe it or not, your experiences in life make you unique and we can use this uniqueness to spark our inner flame. You will find that the more positive you are, the better you will feel as a person and you can start to be proud as you start to work on the future.

You should always try to turn your negatives into positives, but how about turning your negatives into something creative? If you've got this far, you're ready for anything.

Here are eight ways of turning your negative feelings or reactions into something creative and positive:
- When you feel stressed, anxious or depressed, write down your causes and triggers. Use them to write a blog post or article to explain your feelings and how you coped.
- Many people use art as a way to cope and you can create something special even if drawing isn't your thing. If you feel negative, you can take yourself off to a quiet space. You can draw pictures if you like art, or you can simply color mandalas.
- Write a story, song or poem that embodies how you feel or what you know. People will find characters realistic if they are relatable, and poetry is often at its best if it's filled with emotion.
- If you're feeling negative, take some time to meditate or relax. Take a deep breath, close your eyes and think about the negative feelings or actions in your mind and then counter them with a positive statement. Write them down and create mantras and affirmations. You could even stick them around your home or office or create a book full of them.

- Dancing is a great way to express yourself. Put on a song that makes you happy and dance.
- Celebrate your goals or success stories. We don't celebrate our own achievements enough so do something to celebrate that you wouldn't usually do.
- Help someone else in a similar position. Maybe listen to someone who needs to talk through their problems or speak at a support group to inspire others.
- Be honest about how you feel to get it off your chest and then go for a brisk walk. While you are walking, you should think of five things you are thankful for.

You may even think of your own ideas here, as something positive can always come out of something negative. If we can do something that clears our mind or boosts our confidence, we may even become a little bit bolder and braver. This could instill creativity and ensure success in the future. Be as creative as possible with your ideas and find new ways to embed your core beliefs.

As well as being a talking therapy that works on solving your problems and examining core beliefs, CBT is also a goal-orientated therapy, so goal setting is imperative. Now that you know what the problems are, and you're starting to build a positive and healthy belief system, you are ready to look further into the future.

This will help to enhance your motivation as you will have something to aim for that will improve the way you think, feel and react. *That's why you're still reading, right?* Take a few moments right now to think about your ideal goal. *What do you really want?*

Be bold, brave, creative and confident. Remember, this is the new you!

Chapter 8 – Goal Setting for Greater Good

Are you ready to plan your future? In the previous chapters, we've done a lot of soul-searching by analyzing our problematic areas but now it's time to flip those on their head and start looking to the future. We're going to explore how we can set effective goals together and we'll also look at our ideal goal. But first, it's important for you to know just how goal setting applies in CBT and why it's such a key focus.

Problem Focused and Goal Orientated

The whole aim of CBT is to focus on your problems and it's goal orientated. Although it's classed as a talking therapy, goal setting is instrumental to the recovery and success of the client. It focuses on specific problems and gets you to address them directly by setting goals on how you can overcome them. Your problem can be anything that's making you unhappy in your life, from something that makes you depressed or anxious, to even getting that job of your dreams.

Whatever that problem is, CBT helps you set goals to get what you want and map out how you can get there. In the process, you identify the negative thoughts, destructive behaviors or actions and emotions that are holding you back from achieving your end goal.

There are many benefits of goal setting. To start, it gives you a clearer focus and it also helps you to understand the direction that you're heading in. This means that if you have to make decisions, you have clarity and a better understanding of what you must do. Sometimes, simply having a plan of action so we know how to get out of a certain situation or solve our problems is the key to moving forward. This can be a turning point within our therapy and is instrumental to our recovery.

It's time to spend some time thinking about yourself and focusing on what *you* want in life.

> **Activity 13 – Your Ideal Life**
>
> Before you begin reading, close your eyes and imagine your ideal life.
>
> Focus on it. Visualize it!
> *How do you feel? What changes would you need to make to get there? What problems do you want to overcome? What's your ideal?*
> You can use these probing questions to help you set your goals.
>
> *Write down three things you want to focus on achieving – Keep this for later.

When you begin writing and setting your goals, you will need to break them down into smaller stages or steps to help you stay focused and you will be able to monitor your progress as you start to reach for your overall goal. Taking small steps is often more effective because it makes the change transition smoother, and almost seamless. Keep visualizing your end goals and believe you *can* get there!

Strategy 10 – Positive Prediction Planning

Positive Prediction Planning is a great strategy that will help you get into the right mindset for goal setting. Now that you've focused on your problems, your beliefs and your ideal, you're ready to make some predictions for the future. There's only one rule – they must be positive!

Positive Prediction Planning is based on your problems. You look at your current problems, you identify what you want (your ideal or your goal, based on this particular problem) and then you predict the steps you will need to take to reach your ideal.

Activity 14 – Work towards your ideal life, with Positive Prediction Planning

Predict your future with positive prediction planning. Look at the problems you've noted in your journal and complete the table below to create your five steps to success.

What's the problem?	What do you want?	Prediction Steps to Success
I'm stuck in a job I hate and it's making me feel stressed and depressed.	I want a job that I love and will enjoy.	1. Explore career opportunities 2. Upskill or train in appropriate areas. 3. Look for opportunities and apply for new jobs, that excite me. 4. Prepare for any interviews well and boss it. 5. Get a new job that I want!
		1. 2. 3. 4. 5

You should address at least three problems here from your journal, and you should reflect on your new core beliefs and your ideal, too!

Positive prediction planning is effective at helping you figure out what you want in a positive way. It's instructional and you can certainly use this to help you form your CBT goals. If we have a problem, it's down to us to deal with it and do something about it. It's about taking the problems we face and reframing them into something positive.

Now that we are in a more positive frame of mind, it can be easier to find our focus, which leads us nicely onto our next strategy…

Strategy 11 - Finding your Focus

When you suffer from depression, anxiety disorders and stress, it can be difficult to concentrate on any one thing. That's because our mind circulates our thoughts and feelings, and it can feel quite manic and full on. It causes lack of concentration and if we can't concentrate, there's no way we can think in a rational way. We can only solve our problems and change our beliefs, if we can concentrate on the issues at hand and focus on our resolution. We should always allow time at the end of the day to reflect. This can be another way in which journaling can assist as you can write about your day and empty your thoughts onto a page before you switch off. Many people use this strategy. Even if you have all sorts to write about and it hasn't been a great day, you should always think about the positive things that have happened and really focus on how they made you feel. Be proud of those moments.

The relaxed breathing and muscle relaxation exercises from earlier in this book can help you to find your focus. As can chapter 10, when we cover mindfulness. You should also try this next activity:

Activity 15 – Epiphany Moments

Think about some of the things you would like to change from your day. They could be something negative, but to keep in a positive mindset, we should think of these as our epiphany moments. We'll call these epiphany moments, because when you acknowledge your negatives and think about what you can change, or how they could've been better, it's a light bulb moment, or an epiphany.

You did some work earlier on your ideal life. Remember, this is what you are aiming for. This is now your main focus. Close your eyes and imagine the things you would like to change from the day. They are listed behind each other and they are forming a barrier, but your goal is within your grasp, *how can you overcome each barrier?* Leap over each barrier and grab your goal. *Great, you did it!*

Now, think of how you can prevent those events from occurring again by challenging your feelings, thoughts and behaviors, using your epiphany moments. Reflect on each negative situation from your day, and imagine you handle it differently.

Close your eyes again and replay this out in your head but that you handle this in your ideal way. You're still reaching out for your goal and you're on target – you feel proud. Believe it!

Use positive phrases and say them out loud If 'this' ever happens again, this is how I will respond for a positive outcome.

It isn't healthy to dwell on the past and what you 'should' have done too much, but it's perfectly acceptable to reflect on the past and plan how we would deal with that same situation if it happened again in the future. By doing this, you are preparing yourself for the future AND you are learning along the way. You're learning that the way you reacted, or what you felt, and thought is not how you want to act or behave and with that in mind, you're planning to make that change.

Being able to focus on your thoughts and actions can help us with our future plans, and it can help us determine what we want in life and who we want to be. When our mind is full of everything, including thoughts of regret (because we should've acted differently), it clouds our judgement and it's impossible to think straight.

Finding and regaining our focus allows us to be rational and logical. When you can think and act in such a way, you've adopted a positive mindset, and you're ready to start setting your CBT goals.

How to set Effective Goals

We've already talked about CBT being a goal-orientated therapy, so we need to start thinking about the progress we want to make. It's not always easy to set goals that are personal to us, especially when they relate to our feelings, behaviors and thoughts. Regardless of how we feel, goal setting is vital in CBT and it's something that we must do as objectively as possible.

In order to set goals, you should reflect on your new core beliefs and problems that you have worked on in the earlier chapters. You can also reflect on your work from this chapter.

As you've already done the background work, things should run smoothly. We must approach each of your problems and beliefs in turn. Afterwards, we must reflect on them, their causes and how they make you feel or act.

Once you know your ideal and what you want, you need to think about how you can get there, and this is when you need to start setting goals on PAPER strategy. **PAPER** is the acronym you should use when writing down your goals.

Your goals need to be:
Precise - Your goals need to address the situation at hand, and they need to be precise, so that you are clear on what you need to do exactly.
Attainable - Your goals need to be attainable. While I believe everyone should aim high, it still needs to be possible.
Proportionate - Your goals need to be proportionate so that you can monitor and measure them. If your goals are in

proportion, it becomes easier to create the steps or stages you need to achieve your overall goal.

Effectively-Timed - Everyone can be eager to achieve their goals, but it is important to give your goal a timescale and it should be effective. For example, it would be no good to expect to start a new job tomorrow if you just applied today. Give yourself enough time, but don't be too evasive.

Rational - It can be difficult to be rational when you are acting or thinking in an irrational or negative way. Your goals need to be real for you and they need to embody exactly what you need to overcome your current thinking patterns.

When you set your goals, you should use the PAPER framework, to ensure you have tangible, clear goals that you can follow and measure.

Top 3 Tips for Goal Setting

Before you set your goals, you need to think carefully as there are some common mistakes and assumptions that people make when goal setting. This can make your goals counterproductive as rather than motivating you, they overwhelm you:

1. Try to use your newly found focus from the last section and create 3-5 goals. Although it's tempting to create lots and lots of goals because we want to do or change so much, this can actually set you back. You

can goal set at any time, so once you achieve one of your goals, think of another.
2. Remember that you don't have to achieve the whole goal at once. Make sure your objectives/steps towards achieving your goal are small and clear. Take it easy, and don't try to run before you can crawl!
3. Remember this isn't a race! Any progress is better than standing still or going back over. Some people stress if they don't make the progress they want in the desired time, but if you're going to stress, it will only hold you back Take some time to relax and refocus. Then you can dust yourself off and try again.

Activity 16 – Set your PAPER goals

Based on your overall problems and beliefs so far, set 3-5 CBT goals using the PAPER framework, and 5 objectives or steps you need to take in order to reach your goal.

GOAL	STEPS/OBJECTIVES
1.	i) ii) iii) iv) v)
2.	i) ii) iii) iv) v)
3.	i) ii) iii) iv) v)
4.	i) ii) iii) iv) v)
5.	i) ii) iii) iv) v)

You should keep your goals somewhere you can access them easily, like your journal for instance. You can note down relevant dates in your diary, and plan how you will achieve your objectives in advance. For example, if you are wanting to overcome a specific anxiety problem, you may plan your exposure planning activities in your journal/diary too, as well as noting down any results, thoughts, feelings or actions.

Objectives can be really useful as they give us the smaller steps we need to succeed. If you have goals in mind that are attached to your problems or beliefs but need to form your objectives/steps to success, targeting your triggers is a great place to start.

Strategy 12 - Targeting your Triggers

CBT involves knowing your what your problems or issues are and adopting strategies to beat them. In order to overcome our problems, we need to acknowledge and target our triggers. We've already discussed triggers, so you will already be aware that when something makes us feel anxious, there is generally an initial trigger that stirs up those feelings. If you target those triggers at the core before they become out of control, you will often find you are pleasantly surprised at the results.

This strategy involves you reflecting on times when you feel bad or react irrationally to something. You need to then dig deeper and consider what caused that to happen. They are your triggers and if you target them, you can prevent a situation or problem from occurring. The idea is to prevent the negative behavior before it reoccurs. This is great if you find yourself falling into repetitive negative thought patterns.

Targeting your triggers means that you assess each individual problem and look at different solutions for each different problem. You may find that for one of your problems, you use the exposure planning strategy, and for another, you use relaxed breathing. So, imagine that one of your problems is that you start the day off worrying; the relaxed breathing exercise when you first wake up would be great to start your day. This would calm you and it could become part of your daily routine. If you suffer with OCD and want to target an aspect of that, then the next part of your day might mean exposing yourself to an event that usually triggers that behavior.

Activity 17 – Targeting your Triggers Technique

You now need to make a note of possible ways to target your triggers. If you find a pattern repeating itself, knowing how to target your trigger can prevent any episode of stress or anxiety.

Problem	Cause/Trigger	How can I target this?	Give yourself some encouragement
Note your problem or negative behavior here	What are the causes or triggers?	Think about how you can target this issue. What's the solution?	Make a positive statement to encourage yourself – you got this!

Targeting your triggers is a powerful preventative method of dealing with your problems. We keep mentioning preparing ourselves, but if you are prepared in advance to deal with those difficult events, you can deal with them in an effective, appropriate way.

Many anxiety disorders can prevent us moving forward in our life and so can stress, or depression. They may have been holding us back for a long time already, and they are certainly responsible for stopping us from achieving our dreams. In order to keep moving forward, we need to be confident. It's only when we've started to make progress with our confidence, that we can start to build on our awareness and assertiveness skills.

It's time to step things up!

Chapter 9 – Other CBT Techniques

We love CBT because it's continuous in our life. We can keep using its strategies in everyday life and it become natural to us. CBT is so much more than therapy and even when you've started working on your problems and beliefs, there are still further CBT techniques you can learn. We are going to review two further techniques in CBT that will empower you and reinforce your confidence.

Assertiveness in CBT

In CBT, it's important to be assertive. Many people confuse assertiveness with being forceful and it's not the same. Being assertive means that you are brutally honest, and you are willing to express your thoughts, feelings and opinions to others. Maybe this doesn't sound like you right now, but this is something that you can work on. Being assertive can be crucial in CBT because it actually helps us to maintain positive relationships with our peers and family members because it opens up communications channels.

If you bottle things up, they become problematic and chip away at us. As a human being, it is our right to voice our opinion, our concerns, and express how we feel. We shouldn't be ashamed of this, as many successful people are noted for being honest, authentic, and for knowing what they want. Yet sometimes, some people shy away from these abilities. This can be due to numerous issues, such as low self-esteem and lack of confidence.

Being assertive actually gives a sense of confidence as it validates our beliefs and opinions. CBT can help us focus on maintaining healthy relationships and being assertive is key to this. A key part of having a healthy relationship is honesty, *but how can we be honest if we can't express how we feel?*

Being assertive can show confidence and self-belief, but that doesn't necessarily mean that we are no longer approachable, or open to new ideas or opinions. When we're assertive, we don't suddenly lose our listening and communication skills. An assertive person is happy to listen and even empathize with another person, but they are not afraid to say what points they agree with and what points they don't agree with.

Being assertive means that we are approachable and open to new ideas or opinions. We accept that we have different opinions to others and are comfortable in our skin, because we promote the notion that it's acceptable to think differently from others and we're not afraid to acknowledge that.

If you aren't very assertive right now but would like to be, there are some things you can do to increase this

Five Top Tips to increase your Assertiveness

1. Actively listen to others.
2. Accept that others may have different opinions and points of view to you.
3. Express your own points of view in a calm, clear and logical way.
4. Remain positive, open and honest throughout your communication.
5. Avoid conflict by problem solving and stay strong, stick to your beliefs. [24]

Just like most CBT techniques and strategies, assertiveness is something we should work on. You could use the exposure planning strategy, and you could respond in an assertive way to a specific situation, by expressing your opinion when you would usually say nothing or very little.

Activity 18 – Reflection

Think of two situations when you weren't assertive and note them in the table below.

Think of how you could've responded or what you could've said to assert your own point of view, in an amicable and kind way. Often, people mistake assertiveness as being forceful and sometimes even rude, but that's not the case. As assertive people, we tell others what we think in a nice way, in a way that respects their point of view but indicates our own perspectives. You have a right to have an opinion.

Event	How could I be more assertive?

Being assertive gives us a sense of empowerment. If you do respond in an assertive way, we can feel a strong sense of achievement and this can boost our confidence further. This means we become braver, and a little bit better in our attitude when it comes to striving for our goals and getting what we want.

Awareness training is another improvement method when it comes to CBT as it can help you strategize and become the person that you want to be.

Awareness Training

Being aware of CBT is important, as in order to use it, you need to have awareness of what it is and how it can help you. By now, the earlier chapters will have already helped you to increase your knowledge and understanding of CBT and the relevant techniques available to you. This means you are already building an awareness of CBT, but it's important to be aware of when you need to use CBT, and also what your triggers are. This means knowing yourself, and your own conditions.

If you are a regular sufferer of anxiety disorders and depression, you will be aware of some of your core beliefs, problems and your triggers. We will discuss 4 steps to awareness training below;

1. **Identifying and Strategizing** - In the previous chapters we've focused on identifying problems, challenging core beliefs, and we focused on goal setting. This means you have already identified issues and have a strategy in place for CBT. If you haven't done this yet, you should list the things that hold you back and imagine your ideal. You should also explore your core beliefs and have created your new core beliefs so that you have a strategy to live by.
2. **Reducing and Relaxing** - Most people start CBT because they are subjected to stressful situations but

to stop the situation exploding or spiraling, you can use relaxation to reduce stress and anxiety. If you can identify those feelings of depression, stress, panic and anxiety before they start, you could relax by using deep breathing techniques (see point 4). Take yourself off somewhere quiet and relax or have a hot, bubble bath.

3. **Testing and Training** - Test and train your brain and mind by practicing the CBT techniques and strategies we've covered in this book so far. Expose yourself to the situations that usually set you off, and journal how you react, now that you're aware of your behavior. See which one works best for you and you can even tweak them so that they suit you specifically. The best CBT therapy is tailored to both the person and the diagnosis.

4. **Relaxing Breathing Techniques** - You could find somewhere quiet, lay down, and take a deep breath in, and then out for as you can and out for as long as you can then repeat for several minutes, until you feel calm. Alternatively, you could use the seven-eleven breathing techniques. In for 7 seconds and out for 11 seconds. Breathing out more than you breathe in can calm you down quite quickly and it reduce stress and anxiety. This means you can think in a more logical way.

Once you've trained yourself to be aware of your behavior and triggers, the easier it becomes to target them and take action. The most important thing at this stage is to remain patient. Not every technique we've covered will be the right technique for you and sometimes finding the remedy or treatment that works best for you takes some time.

Activity 19 – Being Aware

Just take a few minutes to note down some of your triggers and then answer the following questions:

1. Think about how you react when you are triggered – how do you feel, act and think?

2. What can you do to prevent your reaction?

3. Do you ever know in advance when you are going to be triggered, and can you do anything to stop it?

4. Is there anything you can do to avoid reacting in that particular way now that you're aware?

5. How do you think or wish you could respond when triggered in this way?

Sometimes simply being aware can stop us from blowing things out of proportion or can encourage us to think about why we react in a particular way. Just a little awareness can put a thought in our mind, and we can start to consider how we could react differently, subconsciously. Awareness shows we are open minded, and that we've started to accept our thoughts and behaviors. This is a positive step in the right direction.

There are some things to be wary of, even if you already understand and use CBT.
- Ensure you label your healthy and unhealthy emotions clearly.
- Don't lose sight of your end goal.
- Don't be fooled by your feelings or physical reactions.
- Be open minded and willing to try different techniques until you find the one that works best for you.

Being assertive and having a strong sense of awareness is a great way for you to start to explore CBT further. As you start to change the way you think, you can really start to focus on what areas of your life you need or want to improve. Training your mind to be aware is a great step towards changing the way you think, but you may want to stretch that further and look at behaviors too.

The next chapter talks about Mindfulness-based Cognitive Behavior therapy and this can help you to change behaviors while still being mindful. With CBT, it's important to explore different options and strategies to see which ones work for you. Mindfulness is great at calming yourself and your mind, which helps you to process information in a rational way, so it's worth checking out. This is especially if you enjoyed the breathing and muscle relaxation techniques.

Being mindful just means being aware of the way our thoughts, actions and emotions can affect us, and the people around us. It's the next step following awareness training!

Chapter 10 – Mindfulness-Based Cognitive Therapy (MBCT)

Do you sometimes wish you were a little more self-aware? Our mind is a funny thing as it processes information or events quickly, forcing a reaction before we've even had time to think properly. *Wouldn't it be nice to be able to put things into perspective before we reacted?* In this chapter, we're going to explore mindfulness-based CBT.

Mindfulness Based Cognitive Therapy Versus Cognitive Behavioral Therapy

We've explored CBT in detail, and we've touched on mindfulness a little, but *what is it really?*

Mindfulness has similarities to CBT, as it's described as being "a technique in which one focuses one's full attention only on the present, experiencing thoughts, feelings, and sensations but not judging them." (www.dictionary.com, 2019)[25]

Mindfulness-based Cognitive Therapy focuses on cognitive

therapy and mindfulness, rather than the behavioral aspect that we get from CBT. It looks at attitudes and mood which is why it works well for people who find themselves in severe depressive states and suffer from unhappiness regularly. Breathing and meditation is a key component of this therapy.

Mindfulness is about self-awareness in the same way that CBT is, and although CBT is hugely tailored around mindfulness, it does involve some aspects of analyzing and working on those things too, which sometimes means we judge our thoughts and feelings. CBT also focuses on the behavior aspect too and evokes change, whereas mindfulness raises awareness and believes that becoming aware itself can implement the change without forcing it. Both concepts focus on the present and try to implement changes moving forward.

By adding mindfulness to cognitive therapy, we demonstrate an appreciation for ourselves as well as showing flexibility in our thoughts. There is growing evidence to suggest that MBCT can be a beneficial treatment when it comes to mental health issues and it's often thought of being a great self-help tool (Endelman, 2006).[26]

Important ideas in Mindfulness-based Cognitive Therapy

Mindfulness-based Cognitive Therapy focuses on emotions, thoughts and attitudes. Important ideas in relation to MBCT are:

- Building up a tolerance or coping mechanism that allows us to deal with painful situations better.
- Being open and non-judgmental.
- Reaching an enhanced state of awareness.
- Allowing us to gain insight into ourselves and being in touch with how we feel.
- Using meditation techniques to reflect, recover and cope with specific situations. This can promote emotional wellness.
- Incorporating breathing techniques to help us calm down and cope with our feelings and emotions.

Mindfulness-based Cognitive Therapy is aimed at those that suffer from heightened depression regularly and its key components teach clients to make a break from those negative thought patterns and cope better, whilst improving self-awareness.

How does MBCT Work?

The aim of MBCT is to try and prevent relapses of depression. If a person suffers from regular depressive episodes, it's important to try and change this pattern. MBCT focuses on changing your relationship with your emotions. Mindfulness activities, such as meditation can help to create balance and just like CBT, you can start to change your automatic negative thought patterns and replace them with new ones.

MBCT is about creating a routine and adopting mindfulness technique to cope with an overwhelming situation. The hope is that you can replace your negative thought patterns and prevent those feelings of sadness from turning into depression (Psychology Today, 2019)[27].

Problems that may be addressed by MBCT

Much like CBT, mindfulness-based cognitive therapy is mainly used when treating depression, and this includes moods and feelings of sadness It has been recognized to help those suffering from anxiety disorders, relationship issues, pain, stress and substance misuse too. Let's not forget how useful these coping strategies are in relation to panic too.

If you start to feel down, overwhelmed, or you feel a panic attack coming on, the techniques involved in this treatment can actually prevent it from escalating into depression, although this type of therapy is usually suggested under a therapist if you suffer from depressive episodes regularly (usually three episodes or more).

MBCT Techniques and Exercises

Below are some different techniques and exercises that you might want to explore as part of your MBCT routine. Remember, routine is everything, so planning ahead in time to breathe, meditate, or exercise is a great way to start your MBCT treatment.

Breathing Exercises – Before you can meditate, you need to master your breathing. When we breathe, we typically use our chest and we raise it up and down as we inhale and exhale. Breathing from the diaphragm and stomach area is recommended with MBCT and this involves relaxing your stomach and allowing it to rise and fall as you breathe deeply. You may need to practice your breathing, daily, so spend some quiet time focusing on your breathing technique. You can lay back in the chair, close or open your eyes, or you may prefer to lie down.

Guided Meditations – Many people learn to get themselves into a meditative state without being guided, but for beginners, there are many guided meditations you can use online, on channels like Youtube. Often, guided meditations focus on a specific area, but there are ones that focus on sadness and depression. If you're going to try guided meditation, research the different ones available and listen to them for a few seconds until you a find soothing voice. Once you've found the one for you, kickback and relax. You should practice your breathing techniques for a couple of minutes, just before you begin.

Walking Meditation – With any meditation, you need something to focus on and in this case, you focus on your walking. You don't focus on each step or look at your feet, you simply focus on the fact that you are walking. Walking is a great way to clear your mind and because it's exercise, it gives you the opportunity to refocus, and you will feel refreshed.

Yoga Stretches – Yoga is a great exercise for mindfulness, CBT, and MBCT as it is already a meditative exercise. There are different types of yoga, and some are more spiritual than others. Kundalini Yoga is meditation based and involves quite a lot of breathing exercises as well as chanting. You can attend a class, or there are tutorials online too, if you would prefer.

Activity 20 – Be Brave

There are four mindfulness techniques listed above: Breathing Exercises, Walking Meditation, Guided Meditation and Yoga Exercises.

Choose one of them, preferably a technique that you've never tried before (go on, be brave).

Try it as part of your daily routine for 1 week. Remember, now that you are more 'aware' you should be able to monitor this activity and its outcomes independently, so be objective, realistic and open minded.

Monitor your progress:

Date/Day and time	Activity (what did you do?)	Outcomes: (How did you feel? Did it have a positive/calming/motivational impact? Did you do anything that you wouldn't usually do? What could you do differently? How did it help?)

Other techniques from CBT like journaling, are helpful for MBCT. Recording your thoughts shows that you're paying attention to yourself and your needs. It's a form of self-care which we could all do with a little more of.

MBCT is focused a lot more around positivity, so you could also think of some things daily, that you are thankful for (Edelman, 2006)[28]

Benefits of Mindfulness

As mentioned already, being mindful is a way to take care of yourself and this has numerous benefits for your mind and body. This includes:

- Better general health and state of mind.
- Improved concentration levels.
- Insight into one's self and more in tune with emotions.
- Better control of thoughts and the ability to think rationally.
- Stronger problem-solving skills.
- Feeling motivated and positive.
- Decreased stress and anxiety.

Mindfulness Skills

Being mindful helps us to embed many skills that can help us in our life. It can help us to process our thoughts in a more positive way, as maintaining a fit and healthy outlook. As we feel happier and healthier, we take back control of our lives and we are less likely to feel depressed, anxious or stressed.

Mindfulness can help us to appreciate ourselves and understand the importance of caring for our mind and body. When we feel motivated and content, we are able to overcome barriers that hold us back. We can also feel rested and relaxed which helps us to think rationally.

This means that we often live for the moment and live a happy, fulfilling life!

Other Alternative Cognitive Behavioral Approaches

There are several alternative cognitive behavioral approaches that you can consider:

Acceptance & Commitment Therapy - ACT is different to CBT because rather than challenging negative thoughts, it encourages you to accept your thoughts and then you use something called diffusion techniques to help you overcome these thoughts. You use three broad categories of techniques, the first being acceptance, the second is mindfulness, and the third is based on your commitment to your values. Values give us a purpose, allowing us to reflect on what is really important to us in life (Hayes, 2005)[29].

With this type of therapy, you can still set goals to move forward and it's suggested that knowing our values can free you from the stresses in your life.

Dialectical Behavioral Therapy - The main goal of Dialectical Behavioral Therapy is to gain balance as you expose yourself to difficult emotions by recognizing and experiencing them, then you aim to make a positive change to your behavior.

This therapy is closely linked to CBT as you still set goals and it's aimed at people who feel intense emotions and react in a damaging way. The most important thing is to accept yourself and your reactions, and then try to change these negative or harmful behaviors (Mind.org.uk, 2017).

By talking with a therapist, you can gain an understanding of why you feel and act the way you do, which is part of the acceptance process. It's only when you've taken the first step of 'acceptance', that you then become ready to make those positive changes and move forward (Mind.org.uk, 2017)[30].

Meta-Cognitive Therapy - Meta-cognitive therapy was initially designed to treat generalized anxiety disorders. This refers to metacognitions, which are claimed to be the aspect of cognitions that actually control our thinking process. They refer to negative thinking patterns as being Cognitive Attentional Syndrome and they are driven by underlying positive or negative beliefs. The therapy then focuses on challenging and removing the negative beliefs. It can help you gain control of your thoughts by raising awareness and it helps you to cope with negative ideas and thinking patterns. We can be trained to use our metacognitions to retrieve our memories, but they generally operate in the background. By the end of the meta-cognitive treatment, you can have a more flexible response.

There are many different types of therapies, techniques, and treatments when it comes to Cognitive Behavioral Therapy and we've also explored related therapies too. The most important thing is finding an effective treatment or therapy that suits your needs and symptoms. Sometimes, you may wish to try different techniques until you find the one that fits you best.

Once you find the right treatments, techniques or therapies, and you start to make progress, you need to start thinking about integrating CBT into your daily life and maintaining the momentum to ensure you don't slip back into your own ways (Caselli, 2019)[31]

Many people find that in the initial stages of CBT, they need some assistance with the practices and therapies. Sometimes, they even hit a roadblock when they've made some progress. There's no right or wrong time to change your CBT therapy or treatment. Again, this is individual to you, and your needs. In the next chapter, we get a little philosophical as we look at different treatments for CBT and talk through the details of a complete treatment program. We'll also reflect on therapists and how they can help you make progress and move forward.

Chapter 11 - CBT Treatment

In this chapter, we will explore different CBT treatments and answer common questions on CBT methods and therapy sessions. If you're not quite sure if CBT is right for you, this is the section for you. We'll also think about what you should expect.

How will I know if CBT is for me?
You probably won't know for sure if CBT is for you until you start practicing it. There are some indicators that it might be for you, if you resonate with the points below.

CBT may be for you if:
1. *You like to have something to focus on and a clear direction.* CBT is orientated around personal goals that target the problems that you personally identify. If you like to know what you are aiming for and you need key points to focus on, then CBT could be the treatment for you.
2. *You are willing to learn and work on new techniques and methods.* CBT is a huge learning curve. You learn new techniques, about your fears and beliefs

and sometimes you make realizations about yourself that you didn't previously know.
3. *You're ready to work on the present, not the past.* CBT largely focuses on the present and future. As you know from the earlier chapters, you are required to do some digging into your past when you explore your negative core beliefs.
4. *You are ready to make a lifelong change in the way you view life, yourself and others.* CBT isn't a quick, overnight fix. It requires you to carry out self-reflection and a lot of work on yourself. It becomes a new way of thinking, as your thought patterns change and evolve in a positive way.
5. *You are open minded.* It is important to be open minded when it comes to CBT. There are occasions when you might think that specific activities are not for you, are similar to a previous activity, or you might just not want to try them for one reason or another. The best think you can do is swallow your pride and just give it a try. You have nothing to lose and you never know, you might surprise yourself.

You like simple, yet highly effective ways of solving problems. CBT is simple, yet extremely effective. It focuses on resolving issues, beliefs, feelings and thoughts, by targeting negative patterns. There is a lot of research to support CBT methods, some of which we've reflected on in the earlier chapters. Cognitive and behavioral techniques have been used for decades, and it is now a recognized therapy for stress, anxiety disorders, depression and so much more. (Smith, 2018)[32]

Do I need a Therapist?

This is a tough question as only you can make this decision. With CBT the treatment is individual, and people approach it in many different ways. Many people manage CBT alone and are happy with the difference it makes in their lives as they adopt new strategies, but others may struggle. If a person has severe confidence issues, suffers with depression or an extreme form of anxiety (or other issues), they may not be able to start CBT without some help and may opt for a therapist.

There isn't a right or wrong time to choose a therapist with CBT either. Often, people start practicing CBT techniques, but they then become stuck and are unsure of how to move forward. If this is you, then you may find a therapist instrumental in your therapy.

A therapist will challenge you and ask you those awkward questions. They will also challenge you and help you to figure out the best forms for treatment for you. They also hold you accountable, so if you work best in this way, a therapist could be just what you need. The most important thing is to enlist a therapist if you want or need one as you should never be afraid to get the help or assistance you need, whether it's long or short term – your choice!

What Should I Expect on my First Visit with a CBT Therapist?

Your first session with your therapist is really to find out if your therapist is the right fit for you, and you are the right fit for them. It's a time to be really honest, and sometimes in order to feel that way, you need to have a solid connection.

Your therapist will want to know what you expect from the sessions and what aspects of your life (emotions, behaviors and think patterns) that you want to change. They will also want to know about the things in your life that you don't want to change too. It's worth having a think about these and any barriers you feel that you face in your life (that you are aware of). It's worth thinking about these things before your session and you can even make notes.

In order to provide an effective treatment plan, your therapist will want to know about you and your life so that they can see the bigger picture. This means that during your first CBT session, your therapist will ask you a lot of questions, maybe about your personal life, social life, family, work, and education. They might also ask you how you feel about certain aspects of your life too, for example, they could ask if you are happy in your job/relationship? Or if there is anything you would change.

During this initial period, your CBT therapist will be assessing you constantly so that your treatment targets the right areas. This will help you to get the most out of your therapy. The assessment period can last for more than one session. As a goal-orientated, person-focused, therapy, it can take a little time to work out the root cause of your problems and figure out an individual treatment plan or program. (Gray, 2019)[33]

The most important thing is to create a plan that works for you, so be patient!

What Happens in a CBT Session?

CBT sessions are slightly different for everyone but generally, they are a talking-based therapy session. It can take place as a group session or as a one-to-one session and the idea is that you work with your therapist to break down your problems.

During your assessment period, you will set some goals and they will indicate what you want overall and the therapist's aim is to get you on the right path. You may be asked to keep a journal or diary to record your thoughts and actions, especially in the beginning as this will help you to find any recurring patterns. Your therapist will encourage you to lead the way and identify these yourself.

Your therapist will question you, as well as analyzing your thoughts and actions to help you solve your problems. Basically, at first, they will help you evaluate which are rational or irrational patterns. They will then challenge you and help you work out how you can change any irrational, unhelpful or negative patterns.

As mentioned earlier, you will have some end goals already, but you will need to break them down further into smaller steps. This will help you to monitor your progress during the sessions. You will spend some time at the end of your session discussing how you can put your changes into practice, and you may be left with some homework that will help you embed your new processes.

Remember that your therapist is there to support you. Their job is not to force you into doing anything you're not comfortable with. They will ask you the difficult questions and challenge you, and they could even help you unravel why you don't what to do a specific thing. Their focus is to help you make progress, or at least know why you feel or act the way you do, so that you can start to live your best life.

How Long does CBT Last and How Frequent are the Sessions?

It's difficult to put a timescale on CBT sessions because if you are continually making progress, then you may want to continue with the sessions over a longer period of time. Having a therapist not only helps you figure out your problems, but also holds you accountable for your actions.

CBT sessions are tailored for the individual and they typically last anywhere between 30-60 minutes. People generally either choose to have weekly or biweekly sessions with their therapists and while some people may only need 5 therapy sessions, others could have around 20.

If you find that you are getting towards the end of your therapy, but you still feel like you need accountability or someone to chat to from time-to-time, there may be other options. Maybe you could buddy-up with someone and then you can support and motivate each other.

How do I Find the Right CBT Therapist for me?

Finding the right therapist can be daunting. You could be referred through your own doctor, or you could search yourself for a private practice in your local area. The best thing to do when searching is to call them and have a chat about what they can offer you. Some therapists offer a free first session or telephone consultation, so you should take advantage of these offers.

It is extremely important to have a good therapist-client relationship and in order to do so, you need to choose the therapist. While medical professionals may be able to recommend someone to you, it is worth remembering that there are many different types of therapy. Different therapists might specialize in different types of therapy so you should consider this when you are searching for your CBT professional.

A CBT therapist should be qualified to ensure you get the best from your therapy. CBT professionals are usually qualified Counsellors, Psychiatric Nurses, Psychiatrists, or Psychologists. You could also search for a therapist by looking through directories but ensure that they are qualified, accredited, or licensed professionals.

Medical professionals are ultimately the best place to start when searching for a therapist as they can provide you with recommendations for legitimate therapists. You will only truly know if you have found the right therapist when you work with them. At your initial consultation or when you first make contact on the telephone, you should be honest about your needs and expectations. If you need intensive and regular therapy but it turns out your therapist can only fit you in once per month, you're not going to get the therapy you need. You should also discuss costs, payment terms, and ask how long your sessions will last as well as treatment timeframes. You may not know exactly but having a rough estimate is useful.

Why do I Need to have a Good, Collaborative, Therapeutic Relationship with my Therapist?

When you choose a therapist, it is important to set some ground rules and agreements. If you have the right therapist, are clear of what you expect from your therapy, make agreements and set ground rules, to ensure that you get the best possible outcome.

You could be asking yourself, why you need to have a good, collaborative relationship and basically, this is because it will ensure you succeed.

Therapy is not a one-way street, as each person must commit and do their part. If you and your therapist don't have the same goals in mind, don't agree, or aren't committed to the therapy, then your therapy may not be a success. Ensure you are aware of the roles and responsibilities of both the client and therapist. Your therapist is there to hold you accountable, to help and support you. They should help you implement CBT techniques and give you the tools or information you need to change your behaviors. They will have knowledge and experience of many different techniques, but they should also be honest and realistic, while ensuring you stay motivated.

Your therapist is not there to do the work for you or tell you what to do. They can advise and give their opinion, but they want you to take ownership. You both need to have respect for one another and be committed to the therapy. Remember a good therapist will challenge you when and as they feel it's necessary!

Will the CBT Therapist be able to Understand and Appreciate my own Background?

When you first started reading this book, you were asked to remain open minded. Your therapist will (and should) return this – they will be open minded, and they will appreciate your background.

A good therapist will have excellent listening skills and they will come from a therapy related background; maybe they'll be a psychologist, psychiatrist, or counsellor, but they will have trained and specialize in CBT. They will have dealt with various people from a range of backgrounds, and as a professional, they will understand and appreciate you as an individual.

Your therapist will have worked with others previously, with similar problems and they are trained well to help you deal with your thoughts, feelings and actions effectively. They will be non-judgmental, and extremely knowledgeable in their field. Make sure you chat to your therapist and you should also do some background research too. Don't be afraid to check their qualifications, licenses, and other credentials.

Activity 21 – Assess the pros and cons of hiring a therapist

We've established that it depends on the individual, whether or not a therapist is required.

Reflect on your own problems and beliefs with CBT in mind and highlight the pros and cons of having a therapist.

Belief or Problem	Therapist Pros	Therapist Cons

What about medications?

Again, CBT is tailored to the individual so there's no way to answer this. Medication advice should be taken from a medical practitioner only. There are people who are not keen on taking medication, and they've decided to start with CBT. It's good to stay mindful of this and never rule it out. If a medical professional says we need medication, then the chances are, for now, we need it. There are many different points of view when it comes to medication and it is important to remember that if you have been prescribed medication by a medical professional, you should never stop taking this in favor of CBT without seeking proper medical advice from a qualified person. Reducing or increasing medication is dangerous and should only ever be done under guidance from your doctor.

Some people try CBT as an alternative to medication or as well as medication. CBT can work in both cases, and it is possible that CBT can help you reduce your medication in the future, but this should again, be under medical advice. Your doctor only prescribes medication that is suited for you, and we have to remain open minded when it comes to medication as sometimes this is necessary for recovery.

If you start using CBT but think you may still need medication, ensure you seek medical advice as it is really important to ensure you get the help you need (Branch and Wilson, 2012).[34]

Chapter 12 – Maintenance

You're done, you're better, you're cured…

If only!

Now, I know that if you are reading the maintenance stage, then you will have made great progress with CBT and that's great news.

Congratulations!

BUT now the real work begins. It is amazing that you have developed and made the progress you have so far, but you need to embed and refine CBT practices and techniques into your life and ensure you keep up with this positive way of thinking, reacting and feeling.

You have all the tools you need, so now we need to store them in our mind, so that we can utilize them whenever we need them.

How to Maintain Automatic Thoughts and Cognitive Distortions

The last thing we want is for those negative automatic thoughts to creep up on us again. CBT is not something that you should simply stop once you start to see improvements, but something you should continue to do. You should certainly keep working on your think pattern strategies.

Use journaling methods to note down your thoughts and analyze them later. *Are you experiencing any new negative thoughts? If so, analyze it – what was the trigger? Why do you think that?* You can also reflect on old ones. This is great to challenge your automatic thoughts, your beliefs and to challenge your cognitive distortions.

Put your new core beliefs into practice. You should review your new beliefs daily so you can imprint them in your mind. You should build them into everything you do. Use positive statements or affirmations that relate to your core beliefs every morning and repeat them aloud.

Breathing exercises are a great way to calm and clear your mind so that you can calm down or take a moment to process your thoughts in a rational way. We've discussed these already and they can be very effective.

Mindfulness and meditation techniques are great ways to control and maintain your automatic thoughts by helping you maintain a positive outlook that is ready to solve any problems that life throws in your direction.

Activity 22 – Reflect and Think

*Reflect on your problems and beliefs and think about how or why they may need maintaining. Think about if they are long-term or short-term issues and what you will need to do to maintain them using CBT techniques.

Find the Full and Objective Perspective

You should still continue to grow with CBT even when you've achieved your initial goals and one way you can do that is by adopting an objective perspective. This is something that you are aiming towards already, because it changes the way you think. In CBT you are taught to look at things in a logical, unbiased way,

Having a full and objective perspective means that you take an overall view of a situation and your perspective is not clouded by your emotions or how you feel. You should remove yourself from the situation, feeling or thought, and look at this objectively, whilst maintaining an unbiased and non-judgmental point of view.

Emotional Reasoning

CBT is all about reasoning with your own thoughts and figuring them out, so the next step from this is to keep challenging why you feel a particular way. Whenever you feel a strong emotion you should reason with it. *Is it rational or irrational? How is it making you feel? Why? Is that a good enough reason to feel this way?* By doing this, you stop yourself from being able to overreact, and you can take a moment to question and reason with your emotion

Forging New Synapses

You should keep practicing and questioning the way you think, even when you think you've mastered rational thinking in CBT, it's a working progress. A synapse is a way that we receive and send information in our brain. When something is an impulse, it happens quickly which means that they are difficult to control. As you start to reform your thinking patterns, you can start to reprogram your brain. Rather than negative messages, your brain (with practice) will automatically start to forge new messages and eventually, your thinking patterns and synapses will be automatically be positive.

Avoiding Backsliding

For maintenance purposes, you need to monitor yourself so that you don't revert back to your old ways. You don't want that, *do you?* Keep recording your thoughts and challenging anything negative. We all have good days and bad days, which we can accept but you must remember, a pattern is something that recurs. Staying aware of your own thoughts and feelings can just make you a little more thoughtful when it comes to your own reactions. By challenging yourself, you are keeping that sense of motivation.

Keep up CBT

You should never just stop with CBT, simply because you feel you've improved. CBT is a way of life. If you are tired, you should sleep, if you are hungry, you should eat, if it's cold outside, you wear a coat, so in the same essence, if CBT makes you happy and content, why would you stop? You can use that old excuse of not having time, but the question on your lips should be, *how worthwhile is it to stop?* If CBT has improved your life, your motivation, yourself as a person and maybe even your health and happiness, what could happen if you just stop? *Can you afford to?* Mindfulness, breathing techniques, journaling, goal setting, and meditation can actually save us time as we are less likely to feel stressed, procrastinate, and struggle with our motivation. CBT can be life changing, but you should make it part of your life and routine. It's more than just a treatment!

How your New Healthy Brain Functions

Your brain controls how you think, act and feel every day, in fact it controls everything we do and how we do it.

CBT keeps your brain functioning to the best of its ability. You will be sharp and calm, your brain will process thoughts in a clearer way and your thought patterns will be positive.
If you're also getting enough rest, your mood will improve, and you will generally feel happier and motivated.

For the final part of maintenance, you should produce your own personal maintenance plan, to help you continue on your CBT journey:

Activity 23 – Personal Maintenance Plan	
*Create a personal maintenance plan for yourself. *Ensure you set at least three goals on the areas you want to improve or develop further with CBT. *Think about how you will build the steps towards your goals, and your maintenance techniques into your routine.	
GOALS: 1. 2. 3.	
Steps for improvement/maintenance	**How can I build them into my routine?**

Before you finally go it alone, it's important to remember that the CBT strategies we've covered in this book, are only a taste of the benefits that CBT can have on your whole life. As a bonus, there's an extra chapter added to this book that explains how CBT techniques can be used to boost your energy.

Chapter 13–BONUS CHAPTER: Ten Ways that CBT Techniques can be Used to Boost your Energy

Everyone needs an energy boost from time to time, *am I right?*

Cognitive Behavioral Therapy certainly has many fantastic benefits, but one thing we haven't yet focused on is how you can use CBT techniques to boost your energy. We have discussed some of these energy-boosting steps inadvertently, but in this bonus chapter, we will explore how we can use CBT techniques to boost your energy and why they work.

1. Increased motivation

Goal setting can increase our motivation. This is because we are driven towards something, as we have a target that we are aiming for. Imagine we're practicing archery. Our bow is loaded with an arrow and there's a large target in front of us with a big red circle in the center. *Where do we aim?*

We're naturally motivated to aim for the target, of course. If we are motivated, then we are energized, because we're pumped – we want to hit the very center of our target. We can do this!

2. Better sleep and relaxation

Most people will agree, if you've had a good sleep or some time to relax and reflect, we naturally have more energy. Sleep improves our focus and when we are relaxing or sleeping, our subconscious is processing our thoughts, ideas, emotions, actions and events from the day. Our subconscious needs time to turn them over in our mind and make sense of everything. When we've processed everything, we're ready to make decisions or judgements, and we can also process more information without feeling overwhelmed.

3. Less Stress

If you are stressed out, your mood and energy levels are often low. Often, we can't be bothered to do very much as our emotions drain us and fatigue sets in. CBT works to help you reduce the stresses in your life. This will increase your energy levels, so make the most of them by ensuring you still use CBT techniques to maintain your well-being as this can also link to improvements in your general health too.

4. Better coping techniques

If you are using CBT techniques, you will be coping better with the situations that usually act as a blockade against you. You will have already started to embed the coping techniques that work best for you. Now it's time to push them further and use them to boost your energy levels. When you're reasoning with your thoughts, actions or emotions, remind yourself how far you've come. The prouder you feel, the better, now repeat "I'm amazing. I've come so far". *Say it like you mean it!*

5. Mindfulness and Meditation

Mindfulness and Meditation works on your mind and the way you feel about yourself. If you've been using or experimenting with this part of CBT, you will really be able to take energy boosting to the next level. Mindfulness is all about reflection and awareness of one's self, so this really gives you the time to plug your energy levels with positivity. Meditation is an amazing practice for boosting energy levels, so why not put in your ear pods, click onto Youtube and search for *guided meditations to boost energy levels* and you might be surprised with how many options are available to you.

6. Improved self-care

If we are taking care of ourselves, it shows we appreciate

ourselves, and this can boost the way we feel. Self-care is something that many people don't spend enough time on and that's because it's sometimes difficult to recognize our own self-worth. With self-care, we spend time commending ourselves or we could receive a treat as a result. Often, something simple like a hot, peaceful, bubble bath can really help our state of mind and we can feel ready to take on the day ahead. Self-appreciation certainly makes us feel good and helps us to feel worthwhile and energized.

7. Confidence Boost

A confidence boost is a great way to increase our energy levels. Confidence is a state of mind, and it's how happy we are, with the belief we have in our self. Sometimes we don't believe in our knowledge, skills or abilities and these doubts drain our mind. In comparison, when we feel confident, we have the ability to think in a logical and rational way and we are often more capable of making better decisions.

8. Impact and Exercise

It's common knowledge that exercise makes us feel more energized and this has a major impact on our energy levels. CBT suggests low-impact exercise like walking or yoga stretches, and such things can really help you boost how you feel and increase those energy levels. As you get stronger, you might exercise longer or harder and this will boost your energy levels further. Exercise is so important, and it gives us the *feel-good* factor, but we should concentrate on building our strength slowly for both our body and mind.

9. Less self-doubt is a great feeling

If you have less self-doubt because you've solved your problems and changed your thinking patterns, then you will feel a higher sense of belief in yourself. Self-belief and confidence are closely linked, but the more belief you have in yourself, the more likely you are to trust your instincts and decisions. At the beginning of this book, we reflected a lot on how we can be held back by our thoughts, emotions and actions but once you've mastered the art of dealing with those, you can push even further. That's right, it's time to take risks! I'm not talking about risks that can seriously injure you, just maybe something that you've always wanted to do, or something you've never done before because that little voice in your head wouldn't let you. It blocked you. You now believe in yourself; you trust your own judgement and you're ready to try something new. *Exciting, isn't it?* That's your energy levels getting ready because excitement makes us feel happy, ready for anything, and alive.

10. Better General Health

You can't even begin to deny that overall, CBT brings better general health. We feel good in our mind, body and soul, and we want to be healthy. When we start exercising and feeling good, we start to take better care of ourselves. I'm not just talking self-care here, I mean everything. CBT can promote a healthier attitude and a healthier you. It can encourage you to start eating healthier and again, this is down to self-worth as we start to take more pride in ourselves. CBT encourages us to take care of our mind, live our best life, and aim for happiness. It also promotes exercise and meditation and if you incorporate them into your lifestyle, you can easily find that you no longer comfort eat, crave sugar and salt, and indulge in the same fatty or sickly foods we wanted when we felt depressed. Sometimes, if you're depressed you don't eat, but CBT can encourage us to maintain a healthy balance by eating the right foods regularly in order to maintain energy levels. A healthy diet certainly boosts our energy levels and if we have good health, the energy boosts will last longer.

There is no doubt that Cognitive Behavioral Therapy can boost our energy levels, but it's down to the way you use and incorporate the techniques. Ensure that you use the techniques that are most effective for you, and ensure you keep practicing CBT for maintenance after you've achieved your goals. Use the techniques you've been learning to recognize and utilize your newly found energy. You may not have even realized that you had those energy boosts at your fingertips, but don't waste the opportunity and let them go unused.

CBT will work around you as it's a long-term way of life. Keep following and practicing because for you, it means a constant and consistent, better future.

Conclusion

Throughout this book, we've looked at some great CBT strategies. CBT is a very flexible and helpful therapy, that caters to many people. The strategies in this book are known to help with stress, anxiety disorders, and depression. If you have used the approaches in this book, there is no question that they can help you live a happier life.

This book has strategies that can certainly help you, if you are susceptible and open to CBT. The whole aim of CBT is to challenge you, explore problematic areas and beliefs, and to encourage change to any patterns that are leading to your unhappiness or distress.

CBT enables you... It enables you to grow as a person and understand the reasons why we might act, think or feel in a particular way. If the strategies and techniques are used in the most effective way, they can be life changing. However, Cognitive Behavioral Therapy isn't for everyone. It will only work if you WANT the change and are willing (and motivated) to go on this self-discovering journey.

CBT is not a magic formula and obviously, there are

occasions when it doesn't work for a person or isn't enough. You should never ignore your feelings, thoughts and actions, especially if you are a known sufferer of depression, stress or anxiety disorders (and other illnesses discussed in this book), so with this in mind, you should always seek advice from a medical practitioner above anything else.

Cognitive Behavioral Therapy makes you address your problems and maintain a healthy state of mind, so it's certainly worth trying as it can make a big difference to your life by changing your automatic thoughts. People who use CBT have become successful in many aspects of their life, because they've changed their whole thought process and have generally taken a more positive view of life and altered their mindset. This may mean we can become more successful in our career, we become happier with life, and become a better, healthier person. If you think rationally and logically, you can increase your confidence and other people will see this in you.

CBT can certainly help you fulfill your dreams and get that spark back for life. Even if you don't suffer from a diagnosable condition or disorder, you've got nothing to lose by giving it a try and it could help you revaluate your current situations and learn to live a free and happy existence.

The Cognitive Behavioral Therapy Workbook

Make the change!

Activity 1 – Setting up and Using a Journal

In chapter 4 for activity 1, you're asked to set up a journal. To journal, you need a notebook, or online document to record events from your days.

The most effective way to set up a journal is to make it as possible as possible.

In the Workbook...

It's suggested that at the very top of your journal page for each day, you should note down something you are thankful for today, so ensure you leave a prompt at the top of your diary – *Today, I'm thankful for...*

You then need to set up a table of four columns:
Event – So you can note down information about the event that triggered your reaction.
Feelings – How did this make you feel?
Actions – What did you do or how did you act in response to this event?
Thoughts – What thoughts did the event trigger?

You can note down positive and negative events in the table, but you should color-code these (black for negative and green for positive, for instance).

You should also leave a blank space at the end of your page too, so you can make a personal reflection in your journal.

Remember you need to use your journal every day for a number of weeks. You can assess your thoughts after one week and start to work on further CBT techniques, but you should keep on with your journaling and make it part of your daily routine.

On the next page is a journal sample document for you to copy and use and your own leisure.

Journal

Today, I am thankful for...

Events	Feelings	Actions	Thoughts

Personal Reflection

Activity 2 – Making Sense of it all

This activity is from chapter 4 and its aim is to help you make sense of your problems.

Take your journal, and highlight all of the negative thoughts, feelings and actions that you've identified so far.

Make a table:

Event	Feeling/Thought/Action	Cognitive Distortion	My ideal
Ran into someone at a party who used to bully me at school.	Felt angry, upset. Caused me to be snappy with others and leave the party early.	Blaming others.	Not to feel like I've done something wrong and should leave. I want to feel comfortable enough to stay and move on.

You need to note down the events from your journal in your table. You have to note down what you felt, thought and how you acted as a resulted. You then need to categorize the distortion, now above we use blaming others as our cognitive distortion in the example, now this doesn't mean that the bully is blameless.

Bullying is terrible, but for this exercise, if we think it's someone else's fault for the way we act/feel/think then we are blaming others. Maybe it is their fault and that's fine, but this process isn't about them, it's about you right now and how you can make a change. In the ideal part, simply make a comment on your ideal situation. *How did you want to act/feel/think?*

Once you've got them all down on paper and categorized, the fun can begin.

You'll find a blank copy of the above table for you to copy and use for your own leisure.
With this exercise, you start to realise just how your different events and problems affect you, and it really helps you get to the heard of the problem. Once we understand clearly why there is a problem, we are able to really consider what we must do, how and why.

The Making Sense of your Problems Table

Event	Feeling/Thought/Action	Cognitive Distortion	My ideal

Activity 3 – Why?

This activity is from chapter 5 of your CBT book.

Look closely at your cognitive distortions and using the boxes below, make some notes on the following questions as they will help you figure out why you feel the way you do;

What triggered the reaction exactly (something/one you seen, heard, a song perhaps)?

Why do you think you think you reacted in that way?

What's the worst that could happen if you faced this?

What would make the situation easier for you, or ease your worries?

Activity 4 – How to Identify your Bodily Reactions

This activity is from chapter 5 of your CBT book. It's so important to consider your bodily reactions, because sometimes it's not until we really consider this, that we realise what an affect our problems are having on our lives.

Follow the steps below:
1. Reflect back on your journal, and your work from activity 2.

2. Pick 2 or 3 key events that had the most distressing impact on you.

3. Note them down in the boxes below:

Event (what happened?)	How did my body react?

4. Think about this event and focus on how it made you feel, what it made you think and how you reacted. Now, think about how your body reacted and write this down. Did you keep thinking or reliving this event in your head? How long did the reaction last for (minutes, several days...)? Note down your responses.

5. Repeat step 4 for each key event you've noted down.

Sometimes our reactions last for 5-minutes, while others play on our minds and affect us for a number of days or weeks, so it's important to pinpoint this. Maybe it's still bothering you right now – if so, highlight this.

Activity 5 – Assessing and Challenging your Bodily Reactions

This activity is from chapter 5 and it's all about looking at those bodily reactions and making a judgement call. Throughout the course of this activity, you will need to reflect on what you know from activity 4.

*First of all, you need to A*nalyze*
Look for patterns and correlations between the way you think, feel and act, to the way your body has reacted. For example, if you were put in a stressful situation more than once, take yourself back to that day of the event and the days that follow and ask yourself the awkward questions:

How did my body react?	How does that correlate with the next event?
How was my appetite?	How did I sleep?
How was my mood/stress-levels?	Was I depressed/anxious?

Did I feel unwell/tired/unsocial on that day and the days that follow?	Is this normal for me?
How was I the day before this event?	When was I next/last happy?

Make some statements about your reactions to summarize your bodily reactions.

For example, every time I become anxious, I don't sleep and become unsocial, so I shut myself off from the world to regroup my thoughts. OR, every time I'm stressed out, I become moody and lose my appetite for 3 days.

*Challenge Yourself

You have started to recognize that your body reacts in a particular way to certain events. You can use this to your advantage by challenging and targeting your reactions.

If we use one of the examples from above:

Every time I become anxious, I don't sleep, and I become unsocial, so I shut myself off from the world to regroup my thoughts. There are four problems – the anxiousness, the lack of sleep, being unsocial, cutting ourselves off from the world. Why (and other problem questions) is always a good place to start. *Ask yourself why we feel or react in this way? What is it that we fear?*

By asking probing questions, we're challenging our reactions and although this may not remedy the immediate issues, being aware helps because we begin to understand why we react, feel and think in a particular way.

The ABC Model

The ABC model is referred to quite often in your CBT book, so here is the example of the model provided in your book in chapter 5.

	Irrational	*Rational*
A - Activating Event	Failed driving test	Failed driving test
B – Belief	Must pass the driving test on the first attempt.	<u>Would like</u> to have passed the driving test on the first attempt.
C - Consequence	Negative feelings of sadness, depression, anger, worthlessness.	Healthy feelings of sadness, and disappointment. Feeling of determination to pass next time.

Activity 6 – Using the ABC Model Yourself

This activity is in your CBT book from chapter 5. For this activity, you should make your own version of the table above and use some of the events from your journal and assess them, based on the ABC Model. 2-3 events will be sufficient to begin with because for now, we're simply raising awareness of our beliefs rather than changing them.

Detail the activating event and then your beliefs on a rational and irrational level. Be honest with yourself when it comes to your irrational feeling You will already be aware that this is irrational, but you can only challenge this in the future if this you are honest.

You then need to detail the consequences. *What are the consequences of your irrational thought? What are the consequences of your rational thoughts?*

*Repeat this sequence for some of the other events in your journal and then examine your responses in the table. *Can you see how our beliefs hold us back and stop us from moving forward?*

Using the ABC Model

Event 1	Irrational	Rational
A - Activating Event		
B – Belief		
C - Consequence		

Event 2	Irrational	Rational
A - Activating Event		
B – Belief		
C - Consequence		

Event 3	Irrational	Rational
A - Activating Event		
B – Belief		
C - Consequence		

Activity 7 – Self-Acceptance Exercise and Taking your own Advice

This activity is from chapter 6. It's important to be reflective in CBT, so look at your journal and reflect on one mistake you've made, or something about yourself that you don't like. This should be a something that really stands out for you and has instilled some fear. *You never want to experience that feeling, thought or action again!*

Imagine that a friend or family member feels like this or has made this mistake and they're distraught. What advice would you give them?

What mistake have I made?
What advice would I give if a family or friend made the same mistake? – Be as objective as possible.

Activity 8 – Exploring your Core Beliefs

This activity is from chapter 6 of your CBT book. This is a short activity

Activity 8 – Exploring your Core Beliefs
- Note down the situation that caused your initial problem and focus on how you felt or acted. What was the negative aspect?

  _____

- Really think about what this says about you. What do you think it suggests?

  _____

- Keep asking yourself why. Why did I feel like that? Why did I act like that?

  _____

- What do you think others will think about this?

  _____

- Why will they think that? Do you have any proof that people think this or is an assumption?

  _____

- What does this mean about the world or life?

  _____

- Why do you think the world will think or react like this? Again, what proof do you have of this?

  _____

- Look at your beliefs. Are there any common themes? For example, say your beliefs all point to a lack of self-belief, that's your theme. You then need to question why you have this self-belief and form your own probing questions based on your beliefs. When was the last time you really believed in yourself? What happened to make you stop believing in yourself?

  _____

Activity 9 – Plan your Exposure

This activity is from chapter 6 of your CBT book. Remember that exposure planning exposes you to situations or things that usually cause you to react in an irrational way, whether this be the way you think or act.

- Have a look in your journal from the last week, or your ABC Model and choose some regular events that set off your anxiety or cause some discomfort or distress. It must be something that you're willing to confront.

- Look at your notes and really think about how you feel and how you usually respond.

- Think about how you could respond in a rational and better way (how do you want to think, feel, act, next time this happens?).

- What does it suggest about your problems and your core beliefs?

- Make a plan to expose yourself to a situation or event that will spoke this feeling.

Make notes in the box below:

See the example below and then use the template on the next page for your exposure planning:

Triggering event	Exposure activity	Day/time of 1st exposure	Day/time of 2nd exposure	Outcome after 2nd exposure
What event triggers the feelings, thoughts and actions?	*What happened last time? What will you do to avoid or cope with the situation? How?*	*Date and time of exposure activity.*	*Date and time of 2nd exposure activity.*	*How do you feel after the 2nd exposure? Did it get easier? How successful was it? What did you do differently?*
Triggering event	**Exposure activity**	**Day/time of 1st exposure**	**Day/time of 2nd exposure**	**Outcome after 2nd exposure**

Activity 10 – Targeting Negative Belief Statements

We looked at this in chapter 6 of your CBT book. Do you remember the cereal brand example?
In this activity, we're going to challenge our core beliefs, once we work them out. If we go back to the driving test example, when we first looked at the ABC Model:
Belief: I must pass my driving test on my first attempt.

Based on this, our core belief is: *Failure is not an option.* There isn't a law that says we can't re-sit the driving test (or retake any test for that matter). This belief is false, it's irrational and it's unfounded. You need to respond to your core beliefs in a motivational way. Take a look at the example below:

Current Core Belief	Response to this belief
Failure is not an option	*I treat not winning or getting the results I want as a learning curve. Whenever I feel like I've failed or could've done better, I don't give up. I get back up, dust myself off, and feel more motivated than ever to do better next time.*

Think If a family or friend came to you with this belief, you wouldn't say *Sure, you're a failure, that's it for you now.* So, why do we do this to ourselves?
We are often our own biggest critic, when we should be a fan. We have the power to motivate ourselves and to make the change we crave.

Activity:

1. Make a table like the one above and make a list of your core values, assumptions and beliefs (there is a template for you to photocopy on the next page).

2. Get to the heart of your core belief and find out what it really means.

3. Make a positive statement in response to each of these.

4. Display these somewhere you can see them (post it notes on the wall, your notice board, or in the front of diary). You can refer to them whenever you have doubts.

Remember, we formed our belief system in the first place, so we can change it!

Current Core Belief	Response to this belief

Activity 11 – Relax and Reflect

This relaxation activity is in chapter 7 of your CBT book. You should approach this activity with an open mind. Read through the steps below before you begin.

- ✓ Find a relaxed position in either a sitting or laying position. Make sure you don't cross your arms and legs.
- ✓ Ensure you're somewhere quiet. It can be best if you are alone.
- ✓ Close your eyes and listen carefully.
- ✓ Breathe in for 5 seconds through the nose if possible. Hold for 1 second. Then breath out through the mouth for 5 seconds.
- ✓ Repeat the process around 10 times to regulate your breathing – you should be able to hear yourself breathe. Really concentrate.
- ✓ Your arms, legs and head should all feel relaxed and heavy.
- ✓ Fall into a natural breathing rhythm and focus on the breathing and how your chest rises and falls. Do this for a few minutes until you feel calm.
- ✓ When you're ready, open your eyes.
- ✓ Stay in the relaxed position but reflect back on the thing you were doing before the overwhelm kicked in. Give yourself some time to process this idea or thought again.
- ✓ If you start to feel overwhelmed again, return to the breathing technique – in for 5 seconds hold for 1 second, out for 5 seconds.

Make some notes about how you feel in the box below – when you come out of your relaxed breathing, what's the first thing you think about?

Activity 12 – Timed Muscle Relaxation

This activity is in chapter 7 of your CBT book. Time muscle relaxation can be great to help you relax and clear your mind. Read through the steps below and then give it a try. Remember to keep an open mind.

- ✓ Take yourself off to a quiet place, preferably somewhere you can lie down.

- ✓ Set your alarm for either 10 or 15 minutes.

- ✓ Tell yourself what time the alarm will sound – say it out loud and imagine the sound of your alarm in your head.

- ✓ Lay in a relaxed state. Don't cross any part of your body.

- ✓ Start breathing through your nose, in for 5 seconds, hold for 1 second, and out for 7 seconds.

- ✓ This will send a relaxing feeling through your body, allow it to flow from your shoulders, down, until it reaches your fingertips and then down your body to your toes.

- ✓ Your arms will feel heavy and you should continue to breathe, until you are in a fully relaxed state and then you can start to find your own breathing rhythm.

- ✓ Lay, in your relaxed state until your alarm sounds.

- ✓ You may wish to stay down for few minutes and refocus on your problems or issues, or you may just want to collect your thoughts.

- ✓ Take a couple of deep breaths before you sit up and ensure you move slowly, are your own pace.

Activity 13 – Your Ideal Life

This activity is from chapter 8 of your CBT book Before you begin reading, close your eyes and imagine your ideal life.

Focus on it. Visualize it!

How do you feel?

What changes would you need to make to get there?

What problems do you want to overcome?

What's your ideal?

You can use these probing questions to help you set your goals.

*Write down three things you want to focus on achieving – keep this for later.

```
┌─────────────────────────────────────┐
│                                     │
│                                     │
│                                     │
│                                     │
└─────────────────────────────────────┘
```

Keep your vision in your mind!

Activity 14 – Work Towards your Ideal Life, with Positive Prediction Planning

Predict your future with positive prediction planning. This activity is from chapter 8 of your CBT book.

Look at the problems you've noted in your journal and complete the table below to create your five steps to success.

What's the problem?	What do you want?	Prediction Steps to Success
I'm stuck in a job I hate and it's making me feel stressed and depressed.	I want a job that I love and will enjoy.	1. Explore career opportunities 2. Upskill or train in appropriate areas. 3. Look for opportunities and apply for new jobs, that excite me. 4. Prepare for any interviews well and boss it. 5. Get a new job that I want!
		1. 2. 3. 4. 5

You should address at least three problems here from your journal, and you should reflect on your new core beliefs and your ideal, too!

The template for positive prediction planning is on the following page so you can copy the table and keep working on your problems. Working on your problems is an ongoing process, so this activity is something you can use over and over again.

What's the problem?	What do you want?	Prediction Steps to Success
		1. 2. 3. 4. 5
		1. 2. 3. 4. 5
		1. 2. 3. 4. 5

		1.
		2.
		3.
		4.
		5
		1.
		2.
		3.
		4.
		5

Activity 15 – Epiphany Moments

This activity is in chapter 8 of your CBT book. Follow the steps below and try to work out the epiphany moments in your life.

1. Think about some of the things you would like to change from your day. They could be something negative, but to keep in a positive mindset, we should think of these as our epiphany moments. We'll call these epiphany moments, because when you acknowledge your negatives and think about what you can change, or how they could've been better, it's a light bulb moment, or an epiphany.

2. You did some work earlier on your ideal life. Remember, this is what you are aiming for. This is now your main focus. Close your eyes and imagine the things you would like to change from the day. They are listed behind each other and they are forming a barrier, but your goal is within your grasp, *how can you overcome each barrier?* Leap over each barrier and grab your goal. *Great, you did it!*

3. Now, think of how you can prevent those events from occurring again by challenging your feelings, thoughts and behaviors, using your epiphany moments. Reflect

on each negative situation from your day, and imagine you handle it differently.

4. Close your eyes again and replay this out in your head but that you handle this in your ideal way. You're still reaching out for your goal and you're on target – you feel proud. Believe it!

5. Use positive phrases and say them out loud If 'this' ever happens again, this is how I will respond for a positive outcome.

Embedding how you want to react to something using positive phrases is a great way to stay positive and motivated about your future.

Activity 16 – Set your PAPER goals

Do you remember PAPER goals from your CBT book, in chapter 8? Based on your overall problems and beliefs so far, set 3-5 CBT goals using the PAPER framework, and 5 objectives or steps you need to take in order to reach your goal.

You can copy this template and use as you wish for future goal setting:

GOAL	STEPS/OBJECTIVES
1.	i) ii) iii) iv) v)
2.	i) ii) iii) iv) v)

3.	i) ii) iii) iv) v)
4.	i) ii) iii) iv) v)
5.	i) ii) iii) iv) v)

Activity 17 – Targeting your Triggers Technique

Activity 17 is from chapter 8. This activity is important as you need to be aware of, and feel able to target, your triggers.
In the activity, you should make a note of possible ways to target your triggers. If you find a pattern repeating itself, knowing how to target your trigger can prevent any episode of stress or anxiety.

Problem	Cause/Trigger	How can I target this?	Give yourself some encouragement
Note your problem or negative behavior here	*What are the causes or triggers?*	*Think about how you can target this issue. What's the solution?*	*Make a positive statement to encourage yourself – you got this!*

Activity 18 – Reflection Page

This activity is from chapter 9 of your CBT book. Reflection is extremely important because we should have time to consider the things that have happened in our lives.

First, think of two situations when you weren't assertive and note them in the table below.

Then think of how you could've responded or what you could've said to assert your own point of view, in an amicable and kind way. Often people mistake assertiveness as being forceful and sometimes even rude, but that's not the case. As assertive people, we tell others what we think in a nice way. In a way that respects their point of view but indicates our own perspectives. You have a right to have an opinion.

Event	How could I be more assertive?

Activity 19 – Being Aware

This activity is in chapter 9 of your CBT book. Just take a few minutes to note down some of your triggers and then answer the following questions:

1. Think about how you react when you are triggered – how do you feel, act and think?

2. What can you do to prevent your reaction?

3. Do you ever know in advance when you are going to be triggered, and can you do anything to stop it?

4. Is there anything you can do to avoid reacting in that particular way now that you're aware?

5. How do you think or wish you could respond when triggered in this way?

Activity 20 – Be Brave

We have to learn to be brave and face those uncomfortable things in life. It helps us grow! This activity is in chapter 10 of the CBT book.

There are four mindfulness techniques listed above: Breathing Exercises, Walking Meditation, Guided Meditation and Yoga Exercises.

Choose one of them, preferably a technique that you've never tried before (go on, be brave).

Try it as part of your daily routine for 1 week. Remember, now that you are more 'aware' you should be able to monitor this activity and its outcomes independently, so be objective, realistic and open minded.

Activity: *What did you do?*

Outcomes: *How did you feel? Did it have a positive/calming/motivational impact? Did you do anything that you wouldn't usually do? What could you do differently? How did it help?*

Monitor your progress – you can copy this table and use at your leisure:

Date/Day and time	Activity	Outcomes:

Activity 21 – Assess the Pros and Cons of hiring a Therapist

This activity is in chapter 11 of your CBT book. Now, we've established that it depends on the individual, whether or not a therapist is required but it's important that you make an informed decision. A great way to do this is to think about the benefits (pros) or drawbacks (cons)

Reflect on your own problems and beliefs with CBT in mind and map highlight the pros and cons of having a therapist. Make it personal to you!

Belief or Problem	Therapist Pros	Therapist Cons

Activity 22 – Reflect and Think

The reflect and think exercise is part of chapter 12. The idea is to reflect on your problems and beliefs and think about how or why they may need maintaining. Think about if they are long-term or short-term issues and what you will need to do to maintain them using CBT techniques.

Make notes below:

Activity 23 – Personal Maintenance Plan

The personal maintenance plan is part of chapter 12 of your CBT book. This is a really important part of CBT, because you've already practiced CBT, but you want to keep the momentum going. CBT isn't a magic formula, it's a way of life.

*Create a personal maintenance plan for yourself.

*Ensure you set at least three goals on the areas you want to improve or develop further with CBT.

*Think about how you will build the steps towards your goals, and your maintenance techniques into your routine.

You now know how to set effective goals, so it's time to set some new goals for the future.

Keep going – you got this!

GOALS:

1.

2.

3.

Steps for improvement/maintenance	How can I build them into my routine?

Reference List

[1] Albert Ellis Quotes. BrainyQuote.com, BrainyMedia Inc, 2019. https://www.brainyquote.com/quotes/albert_ellis_318498 accessed September 29, 2019.

[2] Mind. (2017). *Cognitive Behavioural Therapy (CBT)*. [online] Available at: https://www.mind.org.uk/information-support/drugs-and-treatments/cognitive-behavioural-therapy-cbt/#.XY6UCkZKjIU [Accessed 27 Sep. 2019].

[3] Dobson, K. (2010). *Handbook of cognitive-behavioral therapies*. 3rd ed. New York: The Guildford Press.

[4] McLeod, S. (2019). *Cognitive Behavioral Therapy*. [online] Simply Psychology. Available at: https://www.simplypsychology.org/cognitive-therapy.html [Accessed 27 Sep. 2019].

[5] Ellis, A. and Dryden, W. (1997). *The Practice of Rational Emotive Behavior Therapy*. 2nd ed. New York: Springer Pub. Co.

[6] McLeod, S. (2019). *Cognitive Behavioral Therapy*. [online] Simply Psychology. Available at: https://www.simplypsychology.org/cognitive-therapy.html Accessed 29 Sep. 2019].

[7] McLeod, S. (2019). *Cognitive Behavioral Therapy*. [online] Simply Psychology. Available at: https://www.simplypsychology.org/cognitive-therapy.html [Accessed 29 Sep. 2019].

[8] McLeod, S. (2019). *Cognitive Behavioral Therapy*. [online] Simply Psychology. Available at: https://www.simplypsychology.org/cognitive-therapy.html [Accessed 29 Sep. 2019].

[9] McLeod, S. (2019). *Cognitive Behavioral Therapy*. [online] Simply Psychology. Available at: https://www.simplypsychology.org/cognitive-therapy.html [Accessed 29 Sep. 2019].

[10] Klear Minds. (2015). *The History of Cognitive Behavioural Therapy (CBT)*. [online] Available at: https://www.klearminds.com/blog/history-cognitive-behavioural-therapy-cbt/ [Accessed 29 Sep. 2019].

[11] Dobson, K. (2010) *Handbook of cognitive-behavioral therapies*. 3rd ed. New York: The Guildford Press.

[12] Klear Minds. (2015). *The History of Cognitive Behavioural Therapy (CBT)*. [online] Available at: https://www.klearminds.com/blog/history-cognitive-behavioural-therapy-cbt/ [Accessed 29 Sep. 2019].

[13] NHS UK. (2019). *Cognitive Behavioural Therapy (CBT)*. [online] Available at: https://www.nhs.uk/conditions/cognitive-behavioural-therapy-cbt/ [Accessed 27 Sep. 2019].

[14] Mind. (2019). *Cognitive Behavioural Therapy (CBT)*. [online] Available at: https://www.mind.org.uk/information-support/drugs-and-treatments/cognitive-behavioural-therapy-cbt/#.XY6UCkZKjIU [Accessed Oct. 2017].

[15] Davro, B. (2019). *Best Picture Quotes and Saying Images about Peace of Mind - Quote Amo*. [online] Quote Amo. Available at: http://quoteamo.com/peace-of-mind-quotes/ [Accessed 27 Oct. 2019].

[16] Ackerman, C. (2019). *25 CBT Techniques and Worksheets for Cognitive Behavioral Therapy*. [online] PositivePsychology.com. Available at: https://positivepsychology.com/cbt-cognitive-behavioral-therapy-techniques-worksheets/ [Accessed 5 Oct. 2019].

[17] Edelman, S. (2006). *Change your thinking with CBT.* London: Vermilion.

[18] Macgill, M (2017) *What is depression and what can I do about it?* In Medical News Today. Available at: https://www.medicalnewstoday.com/kc/depression-causes-symptoms-treatments-8933 [accessed: 5, Oct, 2019]

[19] Effective Child Therapy. (2019). *Cognitive Behavioral Therapy - Effective Child Therapy.* [online] Available at: https://effectivechildtherapy.org/therapies/cognitive-behavioral-therapy/ [Accessed 5 Aug. 2015].

[20] Ackerman, C. (2019). *25 CBT Techniques and Worksheets for Cognitive Behavioral Therapy.* [online] PositivePsychology.com. Available at: https://positivepsychology.com/cbt-cognitive-behavioral-therapy-techniques-worksheets/ [Accessed 5 Oct. 2019].

[21] Ackerman, C. (2019). *25 CBT Techniques and Worksheets for Cognitive Behavioral Therapy.* [online] PositivePsychology.com. Available at: https://positivepsychology.com/cbt-cognitive-behavioral-therapy-techniques-worksheets/ [Accessed 5 Oct. 2019].

[22] Ackerman, C. (2019). *25 CBT Techniques and Worksheets for Cognitive Behavioral Therapy.* [online] PositivePsychology.com. Available at: https://positivepsychology.com/cbt-cognitive-behavioral-therapy-techniques-worksheets/ [Accessed 5 Oct. 2019].

[23] Ackerman, C. (2019). *25 CBT Techniques and Worksheets for Cognitive Behavioral Therapy.* [online] PositivePsychology.com. Available at: https://positivepsychology.com/cbt-cognitive-behavioral-therapy-techniques-worksheets/ [Accessed 5 Oct. 2019].

[24] Betterhealth.vic.gov.au. (2012). *10 tips for being assertive.* [online] Available at:

https://www.betterhealth.vic.gov.au/health/ten-tips/10-tips-for-being-assertive [Accessed 21 Oct. 2019].

[25] www.dictionary.com. (2019). *Definition of mindfulness | Dictionary.com.* [online] Available at: https://www.dictionary.com/browse/mindfulness?s=t [Accessed 22 Oct. 2019].

[26] Edelman, S. (2006). *Change your thinking with CBT.* London: Vermilion

[27] Psychology Today. (2019). *Mindfulness-Based Cognitive Therapy | Psychology Today.* [online] Available at: https://www.psychologytoday.com/us/therapy-types/mindfulness-based-cognitive-therapy [Accessed 22 Oct. 2019].

[28] Edelman, S. (2006). *Change your thinking with CBT.* London: Vermilion.

[29] Hayes, S. (2005). *ACT: Acceptance and Commitment Therapy.* [online] Getselfhelp.co.uk. Available at: https://www.getselfhelp.co.uk/act.htm [Accessed 22 Oct. 2019].

[30] Mind.org.uk. (2017). *Dialectical behaviour therapy (DBT) | Mind, the mental health charity - help for mental health problems.* [online] Available at: https://www.mind.org.uk/information-support/drugs-and-treatments/dialectical-behaviour-therapy-dbt/#.Xa9bxkZKjlU [Accessed 22 Oct. 2019].

[3131] Caselli, G. (2019). *Metacognitive Therapy (MCT): An Interview with Prof. Adrian Wells.* [online] State of Mind. Available at: https://www.stateofmind.it/2012/05/adrian-wells-metacognitive-therapy/ [Accessed 22 Oct. 2019].

[32] Smith, D. (2018). [online] Brightlandhealth.com. Available at: https://www.brightlandhealth.com/single-

post/2018/07/31/Is-CBT-right-for-me [Accessed 21 Oct. 2019].

[33] Gray (2019). *The 1st CBT Session - What To Expect.* [online] Selfgrowth.com. Available at: https://www.selfgrowth.com/articles/the-1st-cbt-session-what-to-expect [Accessed 21 Oct. 2019].

[34] Branch, R. and Willson, R. (2012). *Cognitive Behavioural Therapy Workbook For Dummies, 2nd Edition.* Chichester: John Wiley & Sons.

www.ingramcontent.com/pod-product-compliance
Lightning Source LLC
Chambersburg PA
CBHW020900080526
44589CB00011B/371